SUPER BOWL TRIVIA
75 A TO Z QUIZZES

SUPER BOWL TRIVIA
75 A TO Z QUIZZES

By J. M. Colbert

Tuff Turtle Publishing
Crofton, Maryland

Super Bowl Trivia: 75 A to Z Quizzes

ISBN 0-9653182-1-4

Library of Congress Catalog Card Number 96-90692

Printed and bound in the United States of America

Cover design: Frankie Clarke

FOREWORD

Pete Rozelle did not invent trivia. He merely invented the perfect vehicle for those of us who thrill to trifles, who adore the inconsequential.

It is even a matter of trivia that the Super Bowl caught its name quite by happenstance. It did not happen on a day when Pete was sitting around with George Halas, Vince Lombardi, and Wellington Mara talking about Al Davis' pompadour.

Rather, Lamar Hunt, one of the architects of the AFL-NFL merger, was awaiting the crushing of his Kansas City Chiefs as the first victim of this glorious event in 1967. Just then his daughter skipped by with a hard rubber ball. She bounced it and the object ricocheted off the concrete bound for the heavens.

"What's that?" asked Lamar, according to pro football legend.

"That's a super ball, daddy."

"Super ball?" mused Lamar.

Super ball -- Super Bowl.

And Lamar Hunt had discovered the buzz words that some day would enchant America, cause John Madden to shriek like a brass monkey trapped in Green Bay in January, and ultimately result in an invasion of sports journalists from the entire globe, except Iraq.

Of course, this matter of trivia is so trivial due to its repetition that J.M. Colbert omitted it from the collection of *Super Bowl Trivia*. Instead, it's fresh stuff, material that has eluded the infamous Super Bowl X.

The Super Bowl X, a group of survivors created to perpetuate trivia, consists of the 10 sports journalists -- print branch -- who covered the first XXX Super Bowls.

Grayer now, or balder, we have returned each January to listen to the platitudes of the coaches, examine the psyches of the quarterbacks, and stuff ourselves with Danish pastries, reminiscing all week about Joe Namath.

These survivors are Ed Pope of Miami; Cooper Rollow of Chicago; Bob Oates of Los Angeles; Jerry Izenberg and Dave Klein, both of Newark; Will McDonough of Boston; John Steadman of Baltimore; Norm Miller, ex of New York; Larry Felser of Buffalo -- and this ink-stained wretch from Detroit.

And here is a most terrifying morsel of trivia: Of the Super Bowl X, only one of these sports journalists through XXX Super Bowls has not ever covered his original home team, the team he covered on his daily beat, at the event Pete Rozelle invented and Lamar Hunt named.

That individual is the guy from Detroit, me, and that is a favorite slab of Super Bowl Trivia.

The rest of my favorites follow, as assembled by J.M. Colbert.

Jerry Green, Grosse Point Woods, Michigan
September, 1996

AUTHOR'S NOTES

Every question in *Super Bowl Trivia: 75 A to Z Quizzes* refers to an event in a SB game, or to one of the players, coaches, owners or officials who has been connected with one of the first 30 SB games. The connection may be obscure sometimes, but it's there.

The 75 quizzes, each with 10 questions and answers, include such categories as commercials, movies, and TV shows that featured Super Bowl players; women who have been involved with the event; announcers; and colleges. Most of the topics are self-explanatory. Others aren't that difficult. Relatives refers to brothers, or a father and son, or to some relations who played in Super Bowl games. Rivalries refer to college ball and which college of which rivalry has had more players in SB games. In Xs & Os, you'll find plays that were either unorthodox or didn't go quite the way the chalk diagram indicated they should.

There is even a quiz of bad Buffalo jokes. The Bills probably have been the butt of more jokes than any other team. It should be noted, though that they won more games in the four years they went to the SB and lost, than any team in the NFL. If it's any consolation, the quiz about Jimmy the Greek isn't too kind either.

There are a few quizzes regarding record runs, catches, and passes. You should be able to score big on these quizzes.

Mostly *Super Bowl Trivia* reflects two years of my exhaustive and excessive research into the minutiae that has accumulated over the years.

The questions for each quiz appear on the recto (right hand, odd numbered page); answers on the verso (left hand, even-numbered page). No fumbling through to the back of the book. Now it's time for the kick-off. Pass the beer and chips, please.   J.M. Colbert

ACKNOWLEDGEMENTS

Many thanks go to all the people who've helped me with *Super Bowl Trivia*. Among them are: Joe Horrigan, Curator, Director of Research Information, Pro Football Hall of Fame and two others from the Hall, Saleem Choudhry, researcher, and Tricia Trilli, library clerk; Jay Smith and Steve Wilson, of Sports Tours, Inc.; Robert Paul Apjok Jr.; Dick Arnette; Upton Bell; Andrew Brandner; Keith Card; John Clinton; Scott Crevier; Joe Feltes; Tom Ferguson; John Goodwin; Leslie Graham; Jerry Green; Jeffery G. Hanna; Evan Katz; Hal Kibbey; Bill Ladson; Barbara Lenihan; John Lynch; Ben McDonald; Michele Morris; Mike Pinto; Bret Rachlin; John Ruhaak; Cora Shown; John Silberstein; Pete Silver; Judy Sladky; Walter Smith; Kathryn Sullivan; Rich Tandler; Frank Ward; John Wazowicz; and Patrick W. White.

AFC-NFC
Questions

1. Prior to the latest expansion, San Diego was the 11th of the 14 AFL-AFC franchises to appear in the SB. Which three AFC teams haven't made it to the Super Bowl?
2. What was the score of the first Super Bowl won by the AFL?
3. Which conference, American or National, has won the most SB games?
4. What's the longest streak by either conference?
5. Despite the NFC dominance of the past decade, the AFC held the power before that. How many of the first 18 games did the AFC win?
6. Of the 14 pre-expansion NFC teams, nine teams have been in SB games. What are the five other teams that haven't been in SB games?
7. Which was the first SB game under the official merger of the NFC and AFC?
8. Name the eight original AFL teams.
9. When the NFL and AFL merged, three NFL teams moved into the AFC; which teams were they?
10. During the current NFL winning streak, seven AFL QBs have tried to change the tide. Who are they?

AFC-NFC
Answers

1. Cleveland, Houston, and Seattle.
2. 16 to 7, Jets over the Colts, SB III
3. The NFC by a 18-12 edge.
4. The current one, enjoyed by the NFC of 12 consecutive games.
5. 12, with nine going to the Miami Dolphins, Pittsburgh Steelers, and Oakland/Los Angeles Raiders.
6. Phoenix, Detroit, Tampa Bay, New Orleans, and Atlanta.
7. Super Bowl V, with the Baltimore Colts beating the Dallas Cowboys.
8. The Boston Patriots, Buffalo Bills, Dallas Texans, Denver Broncos, Houston Oilers, Los Angeles Chargers, New York Titans, and Oakland Raiders.
9. The Baltimore Colts, Pittsburgh Steelers, and the Cleveland Browns.
10. Neil O'Donnell (XXX), Stan Humphries (XXIX) Jim Kelly (XXV, XXVI, XXVII, XXVIII), John Elway (XXI, XXII, XXIV), Boomer Esiason (XXIII), Tony Eason (XX), and Dan Marino (XIX).

ALPHABET
Questions

1. Only three players with a last name starting with "U" have played in SB games. One of them is Broncos wide receiver Rick Upchurch who played in SB XII. Who are the others?
2. Only two players with last names starting with "Z" have been on SB teams. Who are they?
3. Only one coach, working for two teams in two different SB games, had a last name starting with the letter "Z." What is his name?
4. Who's the only player whose last name starts with the letter "Q" who's played in a SB game?
5. Only three men have played in the SB with a last name starting with the letter "I." Who are they?
6. Which SB team nickname comes in last alphabetically?
7. Who is the only man whose last name starts with the letter "Y" who has served on a Super Bowl coaching staff?
8. Three SB coaches have last names beginning with the letter "V." Who are they?
9. Who's the safety who was on a roll as MVP of SB VII and who shares his name with a toilet paper brand?
10. Who was the "Y" player, recipient of the 1967 Outland Trophy winner from of USC, who played tackle for the Vikings in their four SB appearances?

ALPHABET
Answers

1. Johnny Unitas, QB for the Baltimore Colts in Super Bowls III and V, and Gene Upshaw, left guard for the Raiders in II, XI, and XV.
2. Carl Zander, a linebacker for Cincinnati in SB XXIII and Godfrey Zaunbrecher, a center for Minnesota who was on the roster but did not play in SB VIII.
3. Bob Zeman coached for Oakland in SB XI, and San Francisco for SB XXIV.
4. Fred Quillan, center for the 49ers in Super Bowl XVI and XIX.
5. New England Patriots' linebacker Brian Ingram, New York Giants wide receiver Mark Ingram, and Dallas Cowboys wide receiver Michael Irvin.
6. Minnesota Vikings.
7. George Young, with the Baltimore Colts in SB V.
8. Al Vermeil, SF XVI; Dick Vermeil, Eagles, XV; Fred Von Appen, 49ers, XIX, XXIII.
9. Jake Scott, Miami Dolphins when Miami beat Washington 14-7, to go undefeated at 17-0 for the year.
10. Ron Yary.

ANNOUNCERS
Questions

1. CBS and NBC carried the first SB game. Who were the CBS announcers?
2. Who were the NBC announcers?
3. Who is the former field goal kicker for the New York Giants who has been the announcer, either as analyst or play-by-play, for 12 SB games, more than any other person?
4. Which was the first SB game carried by ABC?
5. Which twice-winning SB MVP joined Ray Scott and Pat Summerall in the CBS booth for Super Bowl VIII?
6. Which season-perfect QB was in the announce booth with Dick Enberg and Merlin Olsen in Super Bowl XX?
7. Who's the only SB-winning coach to be a regular in the SB broadcast booth?
8. Which 1961 recipient of the Outland Trophy (tackle from Utah State), member of the LA Rams 1967 Fearsome Foursome, and 1982 inductee into the Pro Football Hall of Fame has been an analyst for five SB games?
9. Which 1977 inductee into the Pro Football Hall of Fame has been analyst for six SB games?
10. Who was in the CBS radio booth announcing the SB XXIX game who was also the play-by-play man for CBS for SB III?

ANNOUNCERS
Answers

1. Ray Scott and Jack Whitaker as play-by-play and Frank Gifford as analyst.
2. Curt Gowdy on play-by-play and Paul Christman as analyst.
3. Pat Summerall.
4. Super Bowl XIX.
5. Former Green Bay Packers QB, Bart Starr.
6. Miami Dolphins' Bob Griese.
7. Oakland Raiders coach of SB XI, John Madden, who has been the analyst for five SB games.
8. Merlin Olsen.
9. Frank Gifford.
10. Jack Buck.

ANTHEM/PLEDGE
Questions

1. Which Right Stuff led the pledge of allegiance at Super Bowl III?
2. Who is Leslie Easterbrook?
3. Which author, whose life was portrayed in his biography *If You Could See What I Hear* sang the national anthem for SB X?
4. Which wife of which sports announcer sang the National Anthem at SB XXIX?
5. Which are the six institutions of higher learning that have presented the Anthem?
6. Who are the two country singers who have performed the anthem?
7. At SB XXVI and XXVII, the National Anthem was accompanied by an American Sign Language interpreter. Can you name either of these people?
8. A Big Band singer, and a pianist known for playing Big Band-type standards performed in SB games 11 years apart. Who are they?
9. What was the media stink following the SB XXV National Anthem performance?
10. Which positive-emoting singing group has performed at half-time ceremonies four times?

ANTHEM/PLEDGE
Answers

1.   The crew of Apollo 8.
2.   She was featured on the *Laverne and Shirley* show after it moved to California, and she sang the National Anthem at Super Bowl XVII.
3.   Tom Sullivan
4.   Kathie Lee Epstein Johnson Gifford, wife of Frank.
5.   Grambling University Band (2), Universities of Arizona & Michigan Bands, U.S. Air Force Academy Chorale, Colgate University Seven.
6.   Charlie Pride and Garth Brooks.
7.   Lori Hilary and Marlee Matlin.
8.   Helen O'Connell and Harry Connick, Jr.
9.   It was revealed that Whitney Houston had pre-recorded the National Anthem and lip-synched her performance.
10.   Up With People.

BACKS
Questions

1. Running back Preston Pearson played for three SB teams. Name them.
2. Who was the running back who played in three consecutive Super Bowls between 1972-1974, winning MVP honors in the last of these games?
3. Which Pittsburgh Steelers running back had 34 carries for 158 yards to earn him MVP honors in Super Bowl IX?
4. What do the Bengals running back Marc Logan, the Bear's running back Thomas Sanders, Giants cornerback Mark Collins, the Bills cornerback Clifford Hicks, and the Bills cornerback Thomas Smith have in common?
5. Who was the first back to win the rushing title in regular season and play in a SB?
6. Who was the second?
7. Which New York Jets running back rushed for 121 yards in SB III?
8. What was O.J. Simpson's finest moment on the field in SB history?
9. Which running back was the first to run for two TDs in a SB game?
10. Who was the first AFC running back to run for a TD in a SB game?

BACKS
Answers

1.   Baltimore Colts (SB III), Pittsburgh Steelers (IX), and Dallas Cowboys (X, XII, XIII).
2.   Miami Dolphins' Larry Csonka.
3.   Franco Harris, breaking Larry Csonka's record set in SB VII.
4.   Each wore a jersey number that coincided with the SB game in which they played. Hicks and Logan wore 23, Smith was 28, Collins was 25 and Sanders was 20.
5.   Dallas Cowboys Emmitt Smith in the 1992 season that ended with SB XXVII. He also was named SB MVP for his 30 carries, two touchdowns, and 132 yards.
6.   Emmitt Smith, in the 1993 season that ended with SB XXVIII.
7.   Matt Snell.
8.   When, dressed in street clothes, he conducted the opening coin toss for SB XXVII. Even though Orenthal James Simpson was a USC-Heisman Trophy winner, set numerous rushing titles, and became the second man in NFL history to rush for 10,000 yards in a career, he never played in a Super Bowl game.
9.   Green Bay's Elijah Pitts in SB I, each followed by PATs from Don Chandler.
10.   Matt Snell, SB III, New York Jets.

BAD JOKES
Questions

1.   What is a "Norwood"?
2.   Similarly, what kind of golf club slices to the right?
3.   What do Jimmy Swaggert and the Buffalo Bills have in common?
4.   Why were the Bills distributing SB sideline tickets to abused children?
5.   What do the Bills stand for?
6.   What's the difference between Corn Flakes (pop corn, potato chips) and the Buffalo Bills?
7.   What's the difference between the Buffalo Bills and a dollar?
8.   What is the Buffalo Bills telephone area code and why had it been changed?
9.   How many Broncos does it take to change a flat?
10.   What do the Bills and birthday candles have in common?

BAD JOKES
Answers

1. A field goal thát goes wide, referring to Scott Norwood, whose 47-yard field goal attempt would have won SB XXV for the Bills had it gone through. Despite rumors, Scott did not change his name to Norwide.
2. A nor-wood.
3. They both make 20,000 people stand up and yell, "Jesus Christ!"
4. Because they never beat anybody at the Super Bowl.
5. Boy, I Love Losing Super Bowls.
6. Cornflakes belong in a bowl.
7. You can get four quarters out of a dollar.
8. 044 (0 for four) to match their record.
9. One, but it takes a whole team for a blow out.
10. They both get blown out once a year.

BOOKS 1
Questions

1.   Which Oakland safety wrote *They Call Me Assassin?*
2.   Which former New York Jet cornerback recorded his career in a book entitled *Confessions of a Dirty Player?*
3.   Whose book did George Plimpton co-author with which Packers and Colts center?
4.   Who, with Dick Schapp, wrote *I Can't Wait Until Tomorrow 'Cause I Get Better Looking Every Day?*
5.   Which coach wrote *The Winning Edge?*
6.   Who (was on the roster, but injured, so he didn't play in SB I), with Al Silverman, wrote *Football and the Single Man?*
7.   Which winning QB wrote *[his name]; Time Enough to Win* with Frank Luksa?
8.   Which former SB player & coach wrote an autobiography with Don Pierson?
9.   Which coach and 1996 inductee into the Hall of Fame wrote a football book with Jerry Jenkins?
10.   Which Bears tackle was the main subject in a Brian Hewitt book?

BOOKS 1
Answers

1.   Jack Tatum.
2.   Johnny Sample, who played in SB III.
3.   *One More July*, with Bill Curry.
4.   New York Jets' QB Joe Namath.
5.   Miami Dolphins' Don Shula.
6.   Green Bay Packers' running back Paul Hornung.
7.   Dallas Cowboys QB Roger Staubach.
8.   Mike Ditka, in a book entitled *Ditka: an Autobiography*.
9.   Former Redskins coach Joe Gibbs produced *Joe Gibbs: Fourth and One*.
10.   William Perry in *The Refrigerator & The Monsters of the Midway*.

BOOKS 2
Questions

1.   James T. Olsen penned a 1974 biography about which flamboyant QB?
2.   Which famed coach who made it to the SB with one team and is now trying to do the same with a second wrote a book with Mike Lupica?
3.   Bob Reiss and Gary Wohl authored this book about which outstanding running back from the Steelers?
4.   Hal DeWindt created a book about which Baltimore Colts defensive end?
5.   George Sullivan wrote *Pro Football A to Z: A Fully Illustrated Guide To America's Favorite Sport* in 1975. The year before he wrote about a former QB and Naval Academy graduate. Who is he?
6.   Which University of North Carolina No. 1 draft choice of the New York Giants was the subject of a 1987 David Falkner book?
7.   Smashing records right and left in the second quarter of SB XXII, which QB authored *Quarterback: Shattering the NFL Myth?*
8.   Which two running backs were the subject of the book *Always on the Run?*
9.   Mark Ribowsky wrote this 1991 biography of former Citadel and USC coach, head coach and GM of a four-time SB team. Who was he?
10.   In 1988 this three-time SB referee wrote about pro football as he sees it. Who is he?

BOOKS 2
Answers

1. *Joe Namath: The King of Football.*
2. *Parcells: Autobiography of the Biggest Giant of Them All.*
3. Franco Harris, in a book of the same name.
4. Charles "Bubba" Smith, in a book entitled *Kill, Bubba, Kill.*
5. Roger Stauback, and the book is *Roger Staubach, A Special Kind of Quarterback.*
6. Linebacker Lawrence Taylor, in *LT, Living On The Edge.*
7. Redskins QB Doug Williams.
8. Miami's Larry Csonka and Jim Kiick, written with Dave Anderson.
9. The book's title is *Slick: The Silver & Black Life of Al Davis.*
10. Jim Tunney, in *Impartial Judgment.*

CENTERS
Questions

1. Which center started for the Packers in SB I and then went on to play for the Baltimore Colts in SB III and V?
2. What helmet used to feature a center in its design?
3. Which school did Jets center John Schmitt attend?
4. Who wore number 00?
5. Who's the only center to play in a SB game whose last name starts with the letter Q?
6. Who played the center Hog in the Redskins defense in SB XVII?
7. Who was the starting center for the Chiefs in Super Bowl I?
8. Who's the only Super Bowl center to come out of Holy Cross?
9. What happened when Steeler center Ray Mansfield snapped the ball to punter Bobby Walden in the first quarter of SB X?
10. How many centers have been named to the Hall of Fame?

CENTERS

Answers

1.   Bill Curry, out of Georgia Tech, for the Packers in SB I and the Colts in SB V.
2.   The New England Patriots.
3.   Hofstra.
4.   Oakland Raiders center Jim Otto.
5.   Fred Quillan, center for San Francisco in Super Bowls XVI and XIX.
6.   Jeff Bostic.
7.   Wayne Frazier.
8.   Bruce Kozerski, Bengals, SB XXIII.
9.   Tight end Billy Joe DuPree tackled Walden and recovered the bobbled ball which set up a Staubach to Drew Pearson for a Dallas TD.
10. One, Jim Otto, of the Oakland Raiders in SB II.

CHICAGO BEARS COMMERCIALS
Questions

1. Coach Mike Ditka did commercials for a credit card, a restaurant, a tourism board, a sportswear company and a motivational film for a brewery. Can you name them?

2. QB Jim McMahon did commercials for a sports shoe company, a soft drink company, an auto manufacturer, a magazine, a sunglasses manufacturer, a watch company, and a foot product. Can you name them?

3. Which Bears running back did commercials for Wheaties, Kentucky Fried Chicken, Kangaroo shoes, Hilton hotels, and Energizer batteries?

4. Safety Gary Fencik drove the competition crazy with which automobile company commercial?

5. Which linebacker who recovered two fumbles in SB XX promoted the services of E.F. Hutton?

6. Defensive end Dan Hampton didn't keep quiet for which product?

7. Which Olympic sprinter pitched the word for Ambassador Office Equipment?

8. Offensive tackles aren't known for softness, but this one helped advertise Wonder bread. Who was he?

9. Namath did the stockings, but who advertised Starr Cosmetics?

10. The Chicago "Blues Brothers," otherwise known as the offensive line, did an automobile commercial. For which company?

CHICAGO BEARS COMMERCIALS
Answers

1.   American Express, Ditka's (Chicago restaurant), Chicago Tourist Board, Starter Sportswear, and Anheuser-Busch.
2.   Adidas, Coca-Cola, Hondo, Sports Illustrated, Revo sunglasses, Ebel watches, and Tinactin foot powder.
3.   Running back Walter Payton.
4.   Cadillac.
5.   Mike Singletary.
6.   Walker Mufflers.
7.   Willie Gault.
8.   Offensive tackle Keith Van Horne.
9.   Cornerback Mike Richardson.
10. Chevrolet.

COACHES 1
Questions

1.   Johnny Rauch, as the Oakland Raiders Coach, once played against one of his own players when Rauch was the QB at Georgia in 1948. Who was this person?

2.   Which coach was named Coach of the Year for 1982 after leading the Washington Redskins to victory in SB XVII?

3.   Who was head coach when the Washington Redskins went to Super Bowls VII, XVII, XVIII, XXII, XXVI?

4.   Who was head coach when the Cowboys went to SB V, VI, X, XII, XIII, XXVII, XXVIII?

5.   Who was head coach when the Dolphins played in SB games VI, VII, VII, XVII, and XIX?

6.   Which coach has won the most SB games?

7.   Who was head coach for the New York Giants when they were victorious in Super Bowl Games XXI and XXV?

8.   Who was head coach for the losing Denver teams in SB XII, XXI, XXII, and XXIV?

9.   Which three coaches have each lost four Super Bowl games?

10.   Mike Ditka has been on the coaching staff of two SB winners. Which were they?

COACHES 1
Answers

1. George Blanda was the Kentucky QB who played under Roach at the end of his career, as placekicker and back-up QB for the Oakland Raiders in SB II.
2. Joe Gibbs.
3. George Allen (VII), Joe Gibbs the rest.
4. Tom Landry for the first five appearances, Jimmy Johnson for the last two.
5. Don Shula.
6. Chuck Knoll, head coach of the Pittsburgh Steelers SB teams for games IX, X, XIII, and XIV.
7. Bill Parcells.
8. Robert (Red) Miller for Super Bowl XII and Dan Reeves the rest.
9. Miami's Don Shula, former Vikings coach Bud Grant, and Buffalo Bills' Marv Levy.
10. The Cowboys (XII) and the Bears (XX).

COACHES 2
Questions

1. Buddy Ryan has been on the coaching staff of two SB winners. Which teams are they?
2. Who was the first head coach to take two different teams to the Super Bowl?
3. Two other coaches have been on the coaching staff of two SB team winners. Who are they?
4. Tom Landry took the Dallas Cowboys to five Super Bowls, played pro ball, and was on the coaching staff of which other team?
5. Which coach of the SB winning San Francisco 49ers was the winningest coach of the 1980s?
6. Which head coach put on a bellboy uniform and carried the players' luggage from the bus to the hotel in SB XVI?
7. Who was Don McCafferty?
8. Before Buffalo Bills Head Coach Marv Levy coached four consecutive losing SB teams, he was on the coaching staff for what other losing SB team?
9. Two head coaches have led their team to three SB victories. Who are they?
10. Three men have been on the coaching staff of more than one winning SB teams. Who are they and what teams?

COACHES 2
Answers

1.   The New York Jets, SB III, and the Chicago
        Bears, SB XX.
2.   Don Shula, the Baltimore Colts and the Miami
        Dolphins.
3.   Mike Ditka with the Cowboys (XII) and the Bears
        (XX) and Bob Zeman with the Raiders (XI) and
        the 49ers (XXIV)
4.   The New York Giants, where he was cornerback
        from 1950-1955 (player-coach in 1954-55) and
        defensive coach for the Giants from 1956-59, all
        pre-SB days.
5.   Bill Walsh.
6.   49ers coach Bill Walsh.
7.   Head coach of the victorious Baltimore Colts for
        Super Bowl V.
8.   The Washington Redskins, SB VII.
9.   Bill Walsh of the San Francisco 49ers in SB XVI,
        XIX, and XXIII; Joe Gibbs, Washington
        Redskins, XVII, XXII, XXVI.
10.   Mike Ditka with the Cowboys in SB XII and the
        Bears in SB XX; Buddy Ryan with the Jets in SB
        III and as defensive coordinator for the Bears in
        SB XX; and Bob Zeman with the Oakland
        Raiders in XI and the 49ers in XXIV.

COACHES 3
Questions

1. Don Shula holds the record for the most SB games at six. Which two teams was he coaching and which Bowls did they play?

2. Who tied Shula's record of one team going to the SB five times under the same coach?

3. Three head coaches have taken their teams to four losing SB finishes. Who are they?

4. Name one of the three NFL teams for which Don Shula played?

5. Pete Rozell presented the first (and second) SB trophy to Vince Lombardi, coach of the victorious Green Bay Packers. What was the first game that the cup was called the Vince Lombardi Trophy?

6. Name the man who coached a SB team and played in the NBA.

7. Only one member of two winning SB teams has a last name that begins with the letter Z. Who is he and what teams did he help coach?

8. Tom Landry took the Dallas Cowboys to the SB five times between 197! and 1979. What was their record?

9. Why was the slogan "Win one for Lefty" heard around Chicago in 1983?

10. What was Coach Mike Ditka's position when Papa Bear George Halas hired him to coach the Bears?

COACHES 3
Answers

1.   Baltimore Colts, SB III and Miami Dolphins, SB VI, VII, VIII, XVI, and XIX.
2.   Tom Landry, coaching the Dallas Cowboys in V, VI, X, XII, and XIII.
3.   The coaches of two of the three teams that have each lost four SB games, Marv Levy (Buffalo, XXV, XXVI, XXVII, XXVIII), Bud Grant, (Minnesota, IV, VIII, IX, XI), and Don Shula (Baltimore Colts, III and Miami, VI, XVII, XIX).
4.   Cleveland Browns, Baltimore Colts and Washington Redskins
5.   From SB V on, the prize was called the Vince Lombardi Trophy.
6.   Bud Grant, who coached the NFL Vikings and played for the 1950-51 Minneapolis Lakers.
7.   Bob Zeman with the Oakland Raiders, SB XI, and the San Francisco 49ers, SB XXIV.
8.   Two wins, three losses.
9.   Because coach Mike Ditka broke his right hand punching a file cabinet after a Bears loss.
10.   Ditka was Cowboys special teams coach.

COACHES 4
Questions

1. Six coaches of SB participating teams are in the Football Hall of Fame. Who are they and what were their teams?

2. One of the first two SB players inducted into the Hall of Fame in 1977 was a QB who played for and then coached the Packers (although not for one of their SB games). Who was he?

3. Green Bay Packers coach Vince Lombardi was presented the first "Super Bowl" championship trophy. Who presented it to him?

4. Cowboys coach Tom Landry, from start to 1988, took his team to the SB five times. What was his record during their first four seasons and what was their final record?

5. Which All-Pro lineman of the Green Bay Packers who played in SB I and II went on to coach a SB team? Which team and which SB?

6. What non-traditional garb did Coach Hank Stram issue to his Kansas City Chief players just before SB I and why?

7. What position and for which team did Coach Mike Ditka play?

8. This coach of the losing '81 SB game is now talking sports. Who is he?

9. Which two coaches faced each other in the first SB game?

10. Who was the first coach to lose two SB games, back to back?

COACHES 4
Answers

1. Bud Grant (Vikings), Weeb Ewbank (Colts and Jets), Chuck Noll (Steelers), Vince Lombardi (Packers and Redskins), Tom Landry (Cowboys), and Bill Walsh (49ers).
2. Bart Starr.
3. Football commissioner Pete Rozelle. From SB V on, the prize was called the Vince Lombardi Trophy.
4. The Cowboys managed only 14 wins in their first four seasons. His final record was 270 wins, 178 losses, and 6 ties.
5. Forrest Gregg, Cincinnati Bengals, SB XVI.
6. Mickey Mouse ears accompanied by the Mickey Mouse theme song. For seven years, the teams in the AFL had been referred to as a Mickey Mouse league and every note taunted them about the sneers they'd heard from the NFL. Alas, it was to no avail as the Green Bay Packers won the game.
7. Tight end for the Cowboys in SB V and VI.
8. Dick Vermeil, appeared on ABC's pre-game show, was coach of the losing Eagles in SB XV.
9. Vince Lombardi and Hank Stram.
10. Bud Grant, coach of the Vikings, in SB games VIII and IX.

COACHES 5
Questions

1. What do coaches Jimmy Johnson, Tom Landry, Vince Lombardi, Don Shula, and Bill Walsh have in common?

2. Tom Flores and Mike Ditka have played on and coached SB teams. Which teams?

3. Although the Redskins fell to the Dolphins in SB VII, George Allen's impact has been felt through his players and coaching staff. In addition to Mike McCormack (Eagles), Jack Pardee (Bears, Redskins, Oilers), and Richie Petitbon (Redskins), three others went to coaching careers with a SB participating team. Who are they?

4. Before Vince Lombardi took the helm at Green Bay, he was on the coaching staff on the college level and with a pro team. Which teams were they?

5. Who was the first coach to win two SB games, back-to-back twice?

6. Who replaced John Madden as head coach of the Oakland Raiders?

7. How many SB rings did John Madden garner as head coach of the Raiders?

8. How many SB rings did Tom Flores win as Head Coach of the Raiders?

9. Which team was Weeb Ewbank coaching prior to his job with the SB victorious New York Jets?

10. Bob Zeman has been on the coaching staff of two SB winning teams. Which are they?

COACHES 5
Answers

1.   Each has a street named after him.

2.   Tom Flores was a QB for the Chiefs in SB IV
      (but didn't play in the game), an assistant coach
      with the Raiders in SB XI, Raiders head coach for
      SB XV and SB XVIII. Ditka was a tight end for
      the Cowboys in SB V and VI, on the Cowboys
      coaching staff for X, XII and XIII, and coach of
      the Bears for SB XX.

3.   Ted Marchibroda (Buffalo XXV, XXVI), Sam
      Wyche (San Francisco XVI and Cincinnati XXIII)
      and Marv Levy (Buffalo XXV, XXVI, XXVII,
      XXVIII)

4.   Lombardi became an assistant coach at Fordham,
      the USMA at West Point, and with the Giants.
      He finished his career with the Redskins, for their
      first winning season in 14 years, in 1969.

5.   Chuck Noll, Pittsburgh Steelers.

6.   Tom Flores, who took the Raiders to the SB in XI
      and XVIII.

7.   One, in Super Bowl XI.

8.   Two, one for XV and one for XVIII as the Los
      Angeles Raiders.

9.   Ewbank, coach of the Baltimore Colts, was fired
      from the Colts squad four years after taking them,
      in 1958, to their second championship.

10.   The Oakland Raiders (XI) and the San Francisco
      49ers (XXIV).

COIN TOSS
Questions

1. Officials conducted the coin toss in games I through XI. Who was the first non-official to toss the coin?
2. Who was the first woman to flip the coin toss?
3. Other than the officials, has anyone conducted the coin toss more than once?
4. Name the United States President who tossed the ceremonial coin for SB XIX.
5. The coach who tossed the coin in SB XIII had a career record of 324 wins, 151 losses and 31 ties and carried the title of "winningest coach" until the '93 football season when Dolphins' coach Don Shula surpassed his record. Who was he?
6. Which MVP from SB I conducted the coin toss for SB XX?
7. Who were the three members of the Miami Dolphins SB teams from VI, VII, and VIII, were bestowed with the coin toss honors in SB XXIII.
8. Which former manager of the Los Angeles Rams conducted the coin toss for SB XXV?
9. Which MVP of SB III was present on the field at the coin toss for SB XXVIII?
10. Who conducted the coin toss for SB XXIX?

COIN TOSS
Answers

1. Red Grange in Super Bow XII.
2. Marie Lombardi, Vince Lombardi's widow, in Super Bowl XV.
3. No.
4. Ronald Reagan, who shared the honors with Hugh (The King) McElhenny, halfback for 49ers, Vikings, Giants, and Lions from 1952 through 1964, before becoming a sportscaster for the 49ers.
5. George Halas, coach of the Chicago Bears.
6. Bart Starr, former QB for Green Bay.
7. Nick Buoniconti, Bob Griese, and Larry Little.
8. Pete Rozelle.
9. New York Jets' QB Joe Namath.
10. Four members of the All-Time team, Otto Graham, Joe Greene, Ray Nitschke and Gale Sayers.

COLORS
Questions

1. Which four-time losing SB team wears purple, gold and white?
2. Which one-time SB champs team wears red, gold and white?
3. Which team, winning one SB and losing one, wore blue and white?
4. Which four-time losing SB team wears blue and red?
5. Which one-time losing SB team wears orange, black and white?
6. Which team, with a 4-1 SB record wears gold and black?
7. Which team, with a 3-2 SB record wears gold and burgundy?
8. Which SB team wore gold and scarlet against another team wearing blue, gold, and white?
9. Which team that wore orange, navy and white defeated a team that wears red, white and blue in SB XX?
10. Which defending SB champs wore green, gold and white against the losing SB team that wore blue, gold and white?

COLORS
Answers

1. Minnesota Vikings.
2. Kansas City Chiefs.
3. Baltimore Colts.
4. Buffalo Bills.
5. Cincinnati Bengals.
6. Pittsburgh Steelers.
7. Washington Redskins.
8. San Francisco 49ers and San Diego Chargers, who met in SB XXIX.
9. Chicago Bears and New England Patriots.
10. The Green Bay Packers and the Oakland Raiders, in Super Bowl II.

COMMERCIALS
Questions

1.   Who lathered Joe Namath's face in the Noxema shaving commercials?
2.   Who was the pitchman for Rolaids antacid?
3.   Besides the famed Coca Cola advertisements, what other product(s) did Pittsburgh Steeler Mean Joe Greene pitch?
4.   Former Oakland Raiders head coach John Madden became a television sports broadcaster and pitchman. For which beer and hardware stores does he do commercials?
5.   Which two former governors did a commercial for Doritos in SB XXIX?
6.   Redskins Joe Jacoby and Darrell Green combined in a DC-based commercial. For what company?
7.   In 1990 Chuck Knox, Art Shell, Dan Henning, Buddy Ryan, Joe Gibbs, and Bill Parcells gathered for a charity program to benefit the Miami Project to Cure Paralysis. What was this losing effort?
8.   49ers QB Joe Montana was also in a shaving commercial, this one for Schick razors. A woman named Jennifer also appeared in the commercial. What happened to her?
9.   Which sports equipment company did Montana do commercials for?
10.   Before he appeared as James Bond, this actor portrayed a 007-type character in a Diet Coke commercial in SB XXI. Who is he?

COMMERCIALS
Answers

1. Farrah Fawcett.
2. Dallas Cowboys Roger Staubach.
3. Swanson frozen Hungry Man dinners and United Airlines.
4. Bud Lite beer and Ace Hardware stores.
5. Mario Cuomo of New York and Ann Richards of Texas.
6. McDonald's Corporation.
7. The six hefty coaches agreed to down ULTRA Slim-Fast diet program and donate $500 for each pound they lost. Five months later they had lost 249 pounds which meant $124,450 to the Miami project. Knox lost the most, going from 236 pounds to 173, for a total loss of 63 pounds. Parcells the least with a mere 32 pounds, going from 265 to 233.
8. The commercial was made in 1984. Montana married her in 1985 and they have four children.
9. L.A. Gear
10. Pierce Brosnan.

DEFENSE
Questions

1.   Who scored the first points for the defense in the Super Bowl?
       a) Willie Wood   b) Mike Bass c) Herb Adderly
       d) Terry Brown
2.   How many times did the Jets defense intercept Baltimore Colts QB Earl Morrall in the first half of SB III?
3.   In SB IV, how many yards did the Kansas City defense allow Minnesota's strong rushing game?
4.   While the Cowboys rushed for a record 252 yards in SB VI, their defense limited the Dolphins to a new record low. What was that figure?
5.   In limiting the Vikings to a measly six points in SB IX the Steelers defense controlled the Vikings game. They also chalked up a new record low number of yards rushing and total offensive yards. What were the records?
6.   How did the Steelers defense strike again in SB X, to defeat the Cowboys by a 21-17 score?
7.   What did Harvey Martin and Randy White do in SB XII to earn co-MVP awards?
8.   The Cowboys defense in SB VI was a determining factor in their 24-3 victory over Miami. How long was the Miami offense on the field?
9.   Who comprised the Killer Bees defense of the Miami Dolphins in SB XVII?
10.   Who comprised the Dolphins No Name Defense?

DEFENSE
Answers

1.   Herb Adderly of Green Bay returned an interception 60 yards for a TD in SB II.
2.   Three times.
3.   67 yards, compounded by three interceptions and two fumble recoveries.
4.   185 yards, while not permitting a Dallas TD.
5.   17 yards rushing, 119 yards total.
6.   The aggressive defense intercepted an end-zone pass on the game's final play.
7.   They led the Cowboys' defense, which recovered four fumbles and intercepted four passes.
8.   20 of the 60 minutes of regulation time.
9.   Bob Baumhower, Doug Beters, Glenn Blackwood, Kim Bokamper, Lyle Blackwood and Bob Brudzinski.
10.   It was led by middle linebacker Nick Buoniconti, and included Jake Scott, Manny Fernandez, Dick Anderson, Vern Den Herder, and Bob Matheson.

DRAFT
Questions

1. Which Baltimore Colts' defensive lineman was the first player taken in the first combined NFL-AFL draft?

2. Raiders Al Davis astounded the experts by using his first draft choice in 1973 to draft a punter from Mississippi State. Who was it?

3. Which University of North Carolina linebacker was the No. 1 draft choice of the New York Giants in 1981?

4. In the 1973 draft, where was Hall of Famer John Hannah picked, and by whom?

5. Which number one prep QB and minor league baseball player was drafted by the Denver Broncos in 1983?

6. Which team originally drafted QB Joe Theismann?

7. His jersey number 11 was retired by the Giants on September 4, 1995. What number was the Morehead State quarterback selected in the 1979 NFL draft?

8. Which North Texas State member of the Steel Curtain was the Pittsburgh Steelers first draft choice in 1969?

9. Which Grambling tackle was the number one draft pick of the Dallas Texans?

10. Which team drafted Lynn Swann, John Stallworth, Mike Webster, Jack Lambert, and Donnie Shell in the 1973 draft?

DRAFT
Answers

1. Charles "Bubba" Smith, the big defensive lineman from Michigan State.
2. Ray Guy, because of his "incredible distance and hang time on his kicks."
3. Lawrence Taylor, who for Christmas one year bought his teammates and the coaches paperweights that looked like SB rings.
4. The Alabama guard, who played in SB XX, was selected as the New England Patriots' top draft choice.
5. John Elway (7) whose five-year, $5 million contract made him the highest-paid player in the NFL.
6. Miami Dolphins, before he reneged on his agreement and signed with the Toronto Argonauts.
7. Phil Simms was the Giants number one pick.
8. Defensive tackle Mean Joe Greene.
9. Junious "Buck" Buchanan, known for his size, strength and agility.
10. The Oakland Raiders.

ELECTED OFFICIALS
Questions

1.   Which defensive lineman for the Minnesota Vikings who played in four SB games (IV, VIII, IX, XI) went on to sit on the Minnesota Supreme Court in 1992?

2.   Who greeted the SB XVII winning Washington Redskins at Dulles International Airport?

3.   What time was it when President Nixon called Don Shula to suggest a down-and-out play?

4.   Which president was supposed to be attending the SB game in the movie *Black Sunday*?

5.   Who was president of the United States when SB I was played?

6.   Who was the first president to make a post-game congratulatory call to the winners in their locker room?

7.   Who was the first president to participate in a SB Coin Toss?

8.   Other than the fact that it was the first presidential coin toss, what else was so unusual about it?

9.   Why were most of the offensive players of the San Francisco 49ers were almost late for warm-ups for SB XVI against the Cincinnati Bengals?

10. Which president had his official swearing-in moved to a Monday, ostensibly to avoid doing so on Sunday, but reportedly because he didn't want to compete against the SB game?

ELECTED OFFICIALS
Answers

1.   Alan Page, out of Notre Dame University, was born in Canton, OH, in the proverbial shadow of the Professional Football Hall of Fame 1988.
2.   President and Mrs. Reagan.
3.   1:30 a.m.
4.   President Jimmy Carter, but it was a look-alike sitting in his place. He did however, become the first president to attend a Monday night football game, in 1978 when he saw the Washington Redskins defeat the Dallas Cowboys, 9 to 5.
5.   Lyndon B. Johnson.
6.   Richard Nixon, who called the Kansas City Chiefs after they defeated the Minnesota Vikings 23-7 in 1970's SB IV.
7.   Ronald Reagan, in SB XIX between San Francisco and Miami.
8.   Reagan did it on live television from the White House in 1985.
9.   Because they were on a bus, due to the snow on the ground around the Pontiac Silverdome, and it was stuck in traffic waiting for Vice President George Bush's motorcade to pass.
10.   Ronald Reagan in 1985.

ENDS 1
Questions

1.   Which defensive end dropped out of pro ball for a year because of a bout of encephalitis, then went on to start all 302 games that the Vikings played between 1961 through 1979, including four SB games?

2.   Who were the two ends who were part of the Washington Redskin "Hogs" offensive line?

3.   Which L.A. Raiders defensive end came out of Rutgers?

4.   Which Miami defensive end stopped a Redskins drive in SB XVII?

5.   Who started as tight end for Dallas in SB VI?

6.   Who was the tight end inducted into the Hall of Fame in 1994?

7.   Which tight end was the first player to earn four Super Bowl rings?

8.   Which tight end played for the Dolphins in SB VII, VIII, and for the Steelers in SB XIII?

9.   Who are the two defensive ends to receive the Super Bowl MVP award?

10.   Which defensive end for the Cincinnati Bengals in SB XVI won the Outland Trophy in 1976 while at Notre Dame?

ENDS 1
Answers

1.   Jim Marshall, from Ohio State.
2.   Don Warren and Rick Walker, each checking in at 6'4" and 245 pounds.
3.   Bill Pickett
4.   Number 77, A.J. Duhe.
5.   Mike Ditka, who also played for the Cowboys in Super Bowl V.
6.   Jackie Smith, who played for the Cowboys in SB XIII, but also played for the Cardinals.
7.   Marv Fleming, playing for Green Bay in SB I and II, and Miami in VII and VIII (he also played for the Dolphins in SB VI, but Miami lost).
8.   Jim Mandich.
9.   Harvey Martin for Dallas in SB XII (shared with defensive tackle Randy White) and Richard Dent of Chicago, SB XXX when he led the defense. that held New England to seven yards rushing.
10. Ross Browner.

ENDS 2
Questions

1.   What do tight ends Greg Latta of the Bears and Brent Jones of the 49ers have in common?
2.   Now that Weber State has been in the NCAA basketball championship and we know how to pronounce the school's name properly, name the Chargers tight end who came out of the school.
3.   Who was the first split end to score a SB TD?
4.   Which onetime Broncos and Raiders defensive end once battled Muhammad Ali in a much-hyped exhibition in Denver?
5.   Which SB featured a TD and a safety scored by defensive players?
6.   How did Steelers defensive end Dwight White prevent a SB record from being set?
7.   Which tight end was the first player to earn four Super Bowl rings?
8.   In what high school sport did 49ers tight end Russ Francis excel?
9.   Who scored the only points in the second period of SB XXI between the Giants and the Broncos?
10.   What school did Eagles tight end John Spagnola attend?

ENDS 2
Answers

1. Both were participants in the Punt, Pass and Kick competition.
2. Alfred Pupunu.
3. Packers Max McGee in SB I, and it was the first TD to be scored in a SB game.
4. Lyle Alzado.
5. SB XX, when Refrigerator Perry scored on a 1-yard run and a safety scored when defensive end Henry Waechter tackled Patriots QB Steve Grogan in the end zone.
6. In SB IX White tackled Vikings QB Fran Tarkenton in the end zone for a safety, the only points scored by either team in the first half, thus assuring that no SB game had had a totally scoreless half.
7. Marv Fleming, playing for Green Bay in SB I and II, and Miami in SB VII and VIII.
8. With a record-setting throw of 259'9," Francis was a superb high school javelin thrower.
9. Giants defensive end George Martin, when he sacked Broncos quarterback Elway in the end zone for a safety.
10. Yale.

FIELD-GOALS
Questions

1.   In SB IV Jan Stenerud of Kansas City kicked what was then a record-setting 48 yard field goal. Who tied that in SB XXI?
2.   Who holds the record for the longest field goal?
3.   Who kicked two field goals thirteen seconds apart for the San Francisco 49ers in SB XVI?
4.   How many field goals did the Vikings score in their four SB appearances?
5.   How much time remained on the clock in SB XXV when Scoot Norwood's 47-yard field goal went astray, thus ensuring the Giant's 20-19 win?
6.   In SB II, Don Chandler kicked four field goals. Who was the only man to tie that record?
7.   Who kicked the 32-yard field goal in the final seconds of SB V to help the Baltimore Colts defeat the Dallas Cowboys?
8.   What is the shortest field goal missed and who attempted it?
9.   Who holds the record for the most field goals attempted in a single game?
10. What was the fewest field goals scored in any Super Bowl game?

FIELD GOALS
Answers

1.   Rich Karlis, in the Denver loss to the New York Giants.
2.   Steve Christie, for Buffalo in XXVIII in the Bills second loss to the Dallas Cowboys, hit a 54 yard field goal.
3.   Ray Wersching, in defeating Cincinnati 26-21.
4.   None.
5.   8 seconds.
6.   San Francisco's Ray Wersching, in SB XVI, in defeating Cincinnati 26-21.
7.   Jim O'Brien.
8.   Mike Cofer missed a 19 yarder for San Francisco in SB XXIII. Rich Karlis, formerly held that record with 23 yards in Denver's loss to the Giants in SB XXI.
9.   Jim Turner of the Jets in SB III and Efren Herrera in SB XII for Dallas, with five each.
10.   Zero, none, zilch, nada. Twice, by Miami and Washington in SB VII and Pittsburgh and Minnesota in IX.

FIRSTS 1

Questions

1.   Which was the first SB defending team?
2.   Which was the first SB with Roman Numerals and why?
3.   Which SB game was the first to be seen by 100,000,000 TV viewers?
4.   Which was the first SB game played at a college campus?
5.   Which was the first SB that ended with those now ubiquitous words "I'm going to Disneyland"?
6.   Which SB game was the first to ask $100 per ticket?
7.   Which was the first SB to pay $38,000 to each member of the winning team?
8.   Which was the first NFC team to win four SB games?
9.   Which was the first team to appear in the SB in three consecutive years?
10. After Green Bay, which was the first team to win a SB game on its first appearance?

FIRSTS 1

Answers

1. The Oakland Raiders.
2. SB V, to avoid confusion of which year the game is played because it is played in January after the previous year's season. Incidentally, Jerry Green, sports writer for the *Detroit News*, was the first writer to refer to the games in Roman numerals. He did this following SB II, in an article for the now-defunct *Complete Sports* magazine.
3. SB XII, and that was just in the United States. About ten times that number watching it world-wide.
4. SB XIX, at Stanford Stadium.
5. SB XXI, and the MVP Phil Simms, uttered that oft-repeated statement.
6. SB XXII. By SB XXX, it was $250.
7. SB XXVIII, Dallas vs. Buffalo. The losers' share was $23,500. In SB I, it was $15,000 and $7,500.
8. The 49ers in SB XXIII. Two AFC teams had done so earlier, the Raiders and the Steelers.
9. The Dolphins in VI, VII, and VIII.
10. The NY Jets, in SB III, against the Baltimore Colts.

FIRSTS 2
Questions

1. Who scored the first SB TD?
2. Which tight end was the first player to earn four Super Bowl rings?
3. Which team was the first to outgain an opponent in total yards from scrimmage but lose the Super Bowl game?
4. Who made the first two point conversion in a Super Bowl game?
5. Which SB saw the first SB mascot?
6. Which was the first, and only, game in which there was a tie for MVP?
7. Where and when was the first indoor SB game played?
8. Which was the first Super Bowl game Gale Gilbert played in?
9. What was the first SB ring made in size 23 and for whom?
10. Which is the first SB game to be tied at halftime?

FIRSTS 2
Answers

1.   End Max McGee of the Packers scored in a 37 yard pass from Bart Starr in Green Bay's 35-10 victory over Kansas City.

2.   Marv Fleming, playing for Green Bay in SB I and II, and Miami in VI, VII and VIII.

3.   The Cincinnati Bengals in their SB XVI loss to the San Francisco 49ers. Bengals had 356 yards to the 49ers 275.

4.   Mark Seay, for the Chargers in SB XXIX.

5.   SB XXIX saw Hosty the Bear. John Routh, who also plays Billy the Marlin for the Florida Marlins and the University of Miami's Maniac and Ibis, filled the costume.

6.   In SB XVI, with the nods going to Randy White and Harvey Martin, Cowboys, for their tremendous pass rushing against the Broncos.

7.   Louisiana Superdome, New Orleans, for SB XII.

8.   SB XXIX, as the Chargers' backup QB. He was on the roster for each of the Buffalo Bills four appearances, but didn't play. He completed 3-of-6 passes for 30 yards and had one pass intercepted in relief of Stan Humphries.

9.   It was made for William "Refrigerator" Perry for SB XX. The average size man's ring is size 11.

10. SB XXIII, with the score knotted at 3-3, between the Bengals and the 49ers.

FUMBLES
Questions

1. In SB XXVI, the Bills had six fumbles which tied the record set by Dallas in defeating Denver in SB XII. Who broke the six fumble record?
2. Which brings us to the question of which game had the most fumbles?
3. What's the record for the most fumbles lost in a single game?
4. Have there been any games without any fumbles?
5. What's the record for individual fumble recoveries?
6. How many fumbles did co-MVPs Harvey Martin and Randy White recover in SB XI?
7. In a game that had the initial appearance of a replay of SB V, the Stupor Bowl, the Cowboys started SB VI with three fumbles in the first quarter, including one on their own one-yard line. How many did they recover?
8. Who was the first player to set a record three fumbles in a single game?
9. Has anyone had the misfortune of matching that record?
10. Which player holds the record for career SB games fumbles?

FUMBLES
Answers

1. Buffalo, again, in SB XXVI, with eight fumbles.
2. Obviously, with Buffalo giving the game a head start with eight fumbles, it was SB XXVI, with a total of 12 after Dallas added the four fumbles they had. The Dallas-Denver game is second, with ten fumbles.
3. Buffalo strikes again, with five in SB XXVI.
4. Yes, three, in SB XIV when LA Rams had no fumbles against Pittsburgh, SB XXIX when San Diego had no fumbles against the 49ers, and in SB XXX when Dallas had no fumbles against Pittsburgh.
5. Mike Singletary, linebacker for the Chicago Bears recovered two fumbles in SB XX against the New England Patriots.
6. Four.
7. All three.
8. Roger Staubach in SB X, when Dallas lost to Pittsburgh.
9. Yes, Jim Kelly in SB XXVI, against Washington; and the next year in SB XXVII when Frank Reich had three fumbles against Dallas.
10. Roger Staubach, Dallas, with five.

GAMES
Questions

1.   Seven players have been in five SB games each. How many, and who, played in all four of the Steelers games?
2.   Which team has been in the most SB games?
3.   Which coach holds the record for the most games as coach?
4.   Which team has been in the most consecutive SB games?
5.   Five of the seven players who've each been in five SB games each played on the Dallas team for those five games. Who are they?
6.   Who are the other two players who've each been to five SB games?
7.   Who are the four head coaches tied with four SB appearances each?
8.   Actually two of those four coaches have been on the coaching staff of another SB team, giving them five games each. Which two and what other team staff where they on?
9.   What's the most consecutive games won by a SB team?
10.   Which team has lost the most consecutive SB games?

GAMES

Answers

1.   None.
2.   Dallas Cowboys, with eight, V, VI, X, XII, XIII, XXVII, XXVIII, and XXX.
3.   Don Shula, with the Baltimore Colts (III) and Miami (VI, VII, VIII, XVII, XIX). Tom Landry is second with five as head coach of the Cowboys (V, VI, X, XII, XIII).
4.   Buffalo, with four (XXV, XXVI, XXVII, XXVIII).
5.   Defensive tackle Larry Cole, safeties Cliff Harris and Charlie Waters, linebacker D.D. Lewis and tackle Rayfield Wright each played five SB games wearing the Cowboys uniform in SB V, VI, X, XII, XIII.
6.   Tight end Marv Fleming with Green Bay (I, II) and Miami (VI, VII, VII), and running back Preston Pearson played for Baltimore (III) and Pittsburgh (IX) before joining the blue, silver and white for X, XII, and XIII).
7.   Minnesota's Bud Grant (IV, VIII, IX, XI), Pittsburgh Steelers Chuck Noll (IX, X, XII, XIV), Washington's Joe Gibbs (XVII, XVIII, XXII, XXVI), and Buffalo's Marv Levy (XXV, XXVI, XXVII, XXVIII).
8.   Noll, who was on the Colts staff for SB III, and Levy who was on the Redskins staff for SB VII.
9.   Two, by Green Bay, Miami, Pittsburgh, San Francisco, and Dallas.
10.   Buffalo, with four.

HALL OF FAME
Questions

1.   Seven SB coaches have been inducted into the Hall of Fame. Can you name them?

2.   Who are the eight QBs, serving on SB teams, who have been voted to the Hall?

3.   Refining that QB list, only one was a number one draft choice. Who was he?

4.   Of the 19 teams that have been in SB games, only two SB team owners are in the Hall of Fame. Who are they?

5.   The 1960s Packers are the only team to have 10 players from a single era in the Hall of Fame. Eight members of the 1970s Steelers comprise the second largest number. Who are they?

6.   The first two SB players inducted into the Hall of Fame were elected in 1977. One was a tackle who played most of his career for the Packers before spending his last (1971) season with the Cowboys; the other was a QB who played for and then coached the Green Bay Packers. Who were they?

7.   Who is the only administrator of a SB team to have been named to the Hall of Fame?

8.   Who is the only placekicker to be named to the Hall of Fame?

9.   Two SB, Hall-of-Fame QBs came from Purdue; two from Alabama. Can you name them?

10.   Between four and seven new members are elected to the Hall of Fame each year. In 1994, six men made it in, two running backs, a coach, a cornerback, a tight end and a defensive tackle. Can you name them?

HALL OF FAME
Answers

1.   Weeb Ewbank, Bud Grant, Tom Landry,
      Vince Lombardi, Chuck Noll, Bill Walsh,
      and Joe Gibbs.
2.   Terry Bradshaw (Steelers), Len Dawson
      (Chiefs), Bob Griese (Dolphins), Joe
      Namath (Jets, Rams), Bart Starr (Packers),
      Roger Staubach (Cowboys), Fran
      Tarkenton (Vikings and Giants), and
      Johnny Unitas (Colts).
3.   Terry Bradshaw (1971) by Pittsburgh, out of
      Stanford.
4.   Lamar Hunt (Chiefs) and Art Rooney
      (Steelers).
5.   Running back Franco Harris, linebacker Jack
      Lambert, owner Art Rooney, QB Terry Bradshaw,
      defensive tackle Joe Greene, linebacker Jack Ham,
      cornerback Mel Blount, and coach Chuck Noll.
6.   Forrest Gregg and Bart Starr.
7.   Tex Shramm.
8.   Jan Stenerud.
9.   Len Dawson and Bob Griese from Purdue; Joe
      Namath and Bart Starr from Alabama.
10.   Running backs Tony Dorsett (Cowboys and
      Broncos) and Leroy Kelly (Browns) Coach Bud
      Grant (Vikings), cornerback Jimmy Johnson
      (49ers), tight end Jackie Smith (Cardinals &
      Cowboys), and defensive tackle Randy White
      (Cowboys).

HEISMAN
Questions

1. There have been five Heisman Trophy winners from military academies including Doc Blanchard, Glenn Davis, Pete Dawkins, and Joe Bellino and a fifth who has played in a Super Bowl. Who is he?
2. Who is the only player to win the Heisman Trophy twice and go on to play in a SB game?
3. Which team did Stanford Heisman Trophy winner Jim Plunkett play for prior to the Raiders?
4. The 1970 Heisman Trophy winner, and the second-highest vote-getter, both went on to QB SB teams. Who are they?
5. What did Joe Theismann do in an attempt to win the Heisman trophy?
6. Which USC Heisman winner, as a SB player had 191 yards on 20 carries (2 TDs, longest run from scrimmage), and received the MVP in SB XVIII?
7. Which Heisman Trophy winner, a running back from South Carolina, went on to play for the Redskins in SB XXII?
8. Which Pittsburgh running back won the 1976 Heisman Trophy, ran for 96 yards in 15 carries in one SB game, and was eventually named to the Hall of Fame?
9. Which USC halfback received the 1965 Heisman and was part of the "offense of the future" for the Kansas City Chiefs?
10. Okay, he never played in a SB, didn't live to see a SB game, so who was Heisman?

HEISMAN
Answers

1. Roger Staubach, 1963 Heisman Trophy winner.
2. Ohio State's halfback Archie Griffin who won the trophy in 1974 and 1975.
3. QB Plunkett played for the Boston (later the New England) Patriots from 1971 to 1976.
4. Jim Plunkett (Oakland Raiders from Stanford) and Joe Theismann (Washington Redskins from Notre Dame).
5. The pronunciation of the Notre Dame QB's name was changed, in a failed effort to rhyme his way into winning the award in 1970.
6. Marcus Allen, for the Oakland Raiders in SB XVIII.
7. George Rogers.
8. Tony Dorsett for the Cowboys, SB XIII.
9. Mike Garrett.
10. John W. Heisman was a college football coach for 35 years from 1892 to 1927. He helped create strategy and revolutionize its rules. Since 1935 the Downtown Athletic Club of NYC has presented an award to the outstanding college football player in the United States. The trophy was named for Heisman in 1936.

INTERCEPTIONS
Questions

1.   The Kansas City 23-7 defeat of the Vikings in SB IV was, in part, due to two fumble recoveries and a number of interceptions? How many?

2.   The interception return-yardage record was set in SB XI. By whom?

3.   The Cowboys converted two interceptions into ten points to a final 27-10 defeat of the Broncos. They also had four fumble recoveries. How many interceptions in total in SB XII?

4.   In SB XIV, how many times was Pittsburgh's QB Terry Bradshaw intercepted?

5.   Who is the only safety who has won the SB MVP award, primarily because of two interceptions?

6.   Who are the two QBs who share the record for the lowest percentage of passes being intercepted in SB career (minimum 40 attempts)?

7.   Which QBs share the record for the most attempted passes without an interception?

8.   Who carries the record for the most interceptions in a single game?

9.   What is the record number of interception by both teams in a single SB game?

10.   How many interceptions did Oakland Raiders linebacker Rod Martin snare in SB XV, returning for 44 yards?

INTERCEPTIONS
Answers

1. Three, one each by Willie Lanier, Johnny Robinson, and Emmitt Thomas.
2. Oakland Raiders' cornerback Willie Brown, made the second of two fourth-quarter interceptions and ran for a record-setting 75 yards to a TD, leading the team to a 32-14 defeat of the Vikings.
3. Four interceptions, one each by Mark Washington, Aaron Kyle, Benny Barnes, and Randy Hughes.
4. The Rams intercepted three times, but Bradshaw brought the Steelers back from behind twice in the second half for a final 31-19 score.
5. Jake Scott of the Miami Dolphins in SB VII, with two interceptions, including one in the end zone to kill a Redskins' drive.
6. With a 0.00 percentage, it's 49er's Joe Montana, 122-0 in 4 games and Oakland's Jim Plunkett 46-0 for two games.
7. Joe Montana, of San Francisco against Cincinnati in SB XXIII, and Steve Young, San Francisco against San Diego, SB XXIX.
8. Craig Morton, of Denver (against Dallas) and Jim Kelly, of Buffalo (against Washington) with four interceptions each.
9. Six, between Baltimore Colts (3) and Dallas Cowboys (3) in SB III.
10. Three, still a SB record.

JIMMY THE GREEK
Questions

1. Who did Jimmy the Greek pick to win in SB III, the Baltimore Colts or the New York Jets?
2. Who did Jimmy the Greek pick to win SB V, between the Baltimore Colts and the Dallas Cowboys?
3. Who did Jimmy the Greek pick to win SB VII, between the undefeated Miami Dolphins and the Washington Redskins?
4. Who did Jimmy the Greek pick to win SB XI, between the Oakland Raiders and the Minnesota Vikings?
5. Who did Jimmy the Greek pick to win SB XIII, between the Steelers and the Cowboys?
6. Who did Jimmy the Greek pick to win in SB XVII, the Washington Redskins or the Miami Dolphins?
7. Who did Jimmy the Greek pick to win SB XVIII, between the Raiders and the Redskins?
8. Who did Jimmy the Greek pick to win SB XX, between the Bears and the Patriots?
9. Who did Jimmy the Greek pick to win SB XII, between the Cowboys and the Broncos?
10. In what year did Jimmy the Greek open his mouth once too often with his theory about genetics?

JIMMY THE GREEK
Answers

1.   The Greek went with the Colts by 18 points. (He wasn't alone; among the fine company he kept was Vince Lombardi, then temporarily retired from coaching who gave the Jets chances of winning as "infinitesimal.") Final score, 16-7, Jets.
2.   The Cowboys, by one. Final score, 16-13, Colts.
3.   The Redskins, by 3. Final score, 14-7, Dolphins.
4.   The Raiders, by 4. Final score, 32-14, Raiders.
5.   The Steelers, by 4. Final score 35-31, Steelers.
6.   The Dolphins, by 3. Final score, 27-17, Redskins.
7.   The Redskins, by 3. Final score, 38-9, Raiders.
8.   The Bears, by 10½. Final score, 46-10, Bears.
9.   The Greek went with the Cowboys, which was right, but by five, which was wrong. The Cowboys triumphed over the Broncos by a score of 27-10.
10. January, 1988, prior to Doug Williams taking the Redskins to victory in SB XXII.

KICKERS
Questions

1. From William & Mary, this kicker set a SB record with his 54-yard kick (his second successful field goal of the day), although his team went on to infamous defeat. Who is he?
2. Who was the first kicker to score five PATs (out of five attempts) in a single game?
3. Among his many achievements, what singular thing has happened to Kansas City Chiefs' kicker Jan Stenerud?
4. The Redskins have this place kicker to thank for their only TD in SB VII. What's his name?
5. What record does Steelers kicker Roy Gerela hold?
6. Who shares the honors for six field goal attempts in two SB games?
7. Which kicker holds the record for the most career field goals completed in SB games?
8. Which 49ers kicker holds the record for most PATs in a SB career?
9. Who was the first kicker to score seven PATs in a single game?
10. Who was the first kicker to score four field goals out in a SB career?

KICKERS
Answers

1.   Steve Christie, kicker for the Buffalo Bills in SB XXVIII, against the victorious Dallas Cowboys, 30-13.
2.   Don Chandler, in SB I between Green Bay and Kansas City.
3.   He's the only kicker to have played in a SB game to have his jersey number, 3, retired.
4.   Garo Yepremian, who tried to recover his own flubbed kick attempt ended up passing the ball into the hands of Redskins' Mike Bass who ran it back for a TD. Dolphins won 14-7.
5.   The most field goals attempted, seven, in his three-game SB career.
6.   Jim Turner, Jets (III) and Denver (XII) and Rich Karlis, Denver (XXI and XXII).
7.   49er Ray Wersching, with five field goals in five attempts in two games.
8.   Mike Cofer, with nine PATs in 10 attempts, in two games.
9.   Lin Elliott, in SB XXVII, Dallas vs. Buffalo.
10.   Don Chandler, in SB I and II, making four out of four attempts.

KICKOFFS
Questions

1. How many yards did Fulton Walker go in his record-setting SB XVII kickoff return?
2. Has anyone matched or bettered that return record?
3. Has anyone else returned a kickoff for a SB TD?
4. Who holds the record for the most kickoff returns in a single game?
5. What's the record for the fewest kickoff returns by one team in a SB game?
6. What SB half was restarted because the network was still in commercial?
7. What's the most kickoff returns, by both teams, in a single game?
8. Who holds the record for the most kickoff returns in a SB career?
9. Who holds the record for the most yards gained from kick-off returns over a SB career?
10. Who holds the record for the most yards gained from kick-off returns in a single game?

KICKOFFS
Answers

1.   The Miami Dolphins cornerback ran back for 98 yards for a TD against the Washington Redskins.
2.   Andre Coleman, San Diego ran back for a 98-yard TD in the third quarter, against the 49ers in Super Bowl XXIX.
3.   The only other player to return a kickoff for a TD in a SB game was Cincinnati's Stanford Jennings, who ran one back 93 yards against the 49ers in Super Bowl XXIII.
4.   Andre Coleman, Denver, with eight, against San Francisco in SB XXIV.
5.   One, in SB III, by the Jets vs. Baltimore Colts; SB XVIII by the LA Raiders vs. Redskins; and SB XXVI, by the Redskins playing against the Bills.
6.   The second half of the first SB game was restarted because NBC was still in commercial.
7.   12, by Denver (9) and San Francisco (3) in SB XXIV.
8.   Ken Bell of Denver, with ten over three games.
9.   Fulton Walker, Dolphins, with 283 yards.
10.   Andre Coleman, San Diego, with 242 yards, in the Chargers losing effort to the 49ers in SB XXIX.

LEFT HANDED
Questions

1.   Who was the first left-handed QB to win a Super Bowl game?
2.   Who was the most recent left-handed QB to win a SB game?
3.   Which left-handed QB shares the record with Joe Montana for the most attempted SB passes without an interception in a single game?
4.   Has any left-handed QB run in for his own TD?
5.   Which left-handed QB has a law degree?
6.   San Francisco and Cincinnati played each other in the SB twice. Who was the left-handed QB for the Bengals for the second meeting, SB XXIII?
7.   Which left-handed SB quarterback was known as The Snake?
8.   Which left-handed QB holds the record for the most TDs in a SB game?
9.   Which lefty QB has the fourth highest record for most yards gained in a game?
10.   Has any leftie won a SB MVP award?

LEFT HANDED
Answers

1.   Oakland Raiders' Ken Stabler, SB XI.
2.   Steve Young, 49ers.
3.   Steve Young, San Francisco against San Diego, SB XXIX, each with 36.
4.   No.
5.   49ers Steve Young, the great, great, great grandson of Brigham Young, has a law degree from Brigham Young University.
6.   Boomer Esiason for Cincinnati.
7.   Ken Stabler, QB for the Raiders. He received his nickname in high school football play.
8.   49ers' Steve Young, with six in SB XXIX.
9.   Steve Young, with 325 XXIX
10.   Yes, Steve Young, in SB XXIX.

MISCELLANEOUS
Questions

1. Who was Sandra Sexton?
2. Has the SB ever had an overtime period?
3. How many players played in all four of the Steelers SB games?
4. Has any team ever been shut out of a SB game?
5. Has any team ever won three consecutive SB games?
6. What do Hollywood Bags, Broke Bird, Whiz Kid and Utah Gold have in common?
7. In how many games did the Vikings have the lead before losing their four SB games?
8. Of the first 30 SB games, how many have had two teams that have never been in a SB before?
9. How many years elapsed between the Cowboys fifth and sixth appearances at SB games?
10. What do 49ers left tackle Steve Wallace and Bengals nose tackle Tim Krumrie have in common?

MISCELLANEOUS
Answers

1. The Bourbon Street strip tease headliner from New Orleans who streaked across the halftime field during SB IX, in her bra and panties.
2. No.
3. 22.
4. No.
5. No.
6. They were the CB handles of L.C. Greenwood, Claude Humphrey, Danny White, and Golden Richards.
7. None.
8. Four, SB I (Packers vs Chiefs), III (Jets vs Colts), XVI 49ers vs Bengals), and XX (Bears vs Patriots).
9. 14, between SB XII (lost to Steelers) and XXVII (defeating Bills).
10. Wallace broke his left ankle on the third play of SB XXIII and Krumrie broke two bones in his leg on the 49ers next series.

THE MOST
Questions

1.   Seven men have played in five SB games. Can you name any of them? One major hint, five of them were with the Cowboys and a sixth was with the Cowboys for three of his appearances.
2.   Who has been head coach for the most SB participating teams?
3.   Which head coach has been the head coach for the most games with a winning team?
4.   True or False: Jerry Rice holds the SB record for most career receiving yards?
5.   Who has the record for the most yards receiving in a single SB game?
6.   Which QB threw for the most TDs in a SB game? a) Terry Bradshaw b) Doug Williams c) Joe Montana d) Steve Young
7.   Two players hold the record for the most receptions in a single SB game. Who are they?
8.   Prior to SB XXIX when San Francisco (7) and San Diego (3) scored a record 10 PATs (including two 2-point conversions), which game(s) held the record for most PATs?
9.   Which player has scored the most points in all the games he's played in? How many points in how many games?
10. Which team has had the most total points scored against them in SB games?

THE MOST
Answers

1.   Marv Fleming, Green Bay I, II and Miami, VI, VII, VIII; Larry Cole, Cliff Harris, D.D. Lewis, Charlie Waters, and Rayfield Wright, Cowboys, Super Bowls V, VI, X, XII, XIII. Preston Pearson, Baltimore Colts, SB III, and Steelers, IX and Cowboys, X, XII, XIII.

2.   Don Shula, with six, for Baltimore Colts, III, and Dolphins VI, VII, VIII, and XVII, XIX.

3.   Chuck Noll, the Steelers, with four, IX, X, XIII, and XIV. Bill Walsh of the 49ers and Joe Gibbs of the Redskins come in second with three each.

4.   True. In three games, Rice has 513 yards. Prior to SB XXIX, Steelers Lynn Swann was leading with 364 yards to Rice's 363 yards.

5.   Jerry Rice, with 215 when the 49ers played the Cincinnati Bengals in SB XXIII.

6.   D) Steve Young with six in SB XXIX against the Chargers, besting Montana's record of five against Denver in SB XXV.

7.   Each has 11 receptions. Dan Ross of the Bengals against the 49ers in SB XVI and Jerry Rice in the repeat match between these teams in SB XXIII.

8.   Two games, SB XIII when Pittsburgh scored five and Dallas scored four, and SB XXVII when Dallas scored seven and Buffalo scored two.

9.   Jerry Rice of the 49ers, in three games, with 42 points.

10.   The Denver Broncos, with 163, in their four SB appearances.

MOVIES 1
Questions

1. Besides watching SB X in Miami's Orange Bowl, the 80,187 spectators did something else on that January 18, 1976 that has them living in history. What was it?

2. Which coach did Ernest Borgnine portray in the made-for-TV movie *Portrait: Legend in Granite*?

3. Which movie featured Dan Marino and some of the Dolphins against the Philadelphia Eagles in a SB matchup?

4. Which product was Marino doing a commercial for when he was kidnapped in that movie?

5. Which 1978 movie featured Warren Beatty in three different roles and how did they pertain to the Super Bowl?

6. Which SB sports commentators appeared in this Warren Beatty movie?

7. Which defensive end played O.W. Shaddock in *North Dallas Forty*?

8. Carl Eller, defensive end for Minnesota Vikings in SB IV, VIII, IX, and XI appeared in which 1974 movie with Elliott Gould and Robert Blake?

9. This Minnesota QB from SB IV days was in this 1974 Burt Reynolds and Eddie Albert football in prison flick. What's the movie's title?

10. *Three the Hard Way*, a nonstop action film featured this Kansas City back from Super Bowl I. What's his name?

MOVIES 1
Answers

1.   They were extras in the movie *Black Sunday*, where
      terrorists were going to attack the stadium via
      blimp. Among those in the flick were Terry
      Bradshaw and Roger Staubach, members of the
      Steelers and Cowboys teams, and Joe Robbie.
2.   Green Bay Packers coach Vince Lombardi.
3.   *Ace Ventura, Pet Detective.*
4.   Isotoner gloves.
5.   *Heaven Can Wait*, where Beatty played Joe
      Pendleton, QB for the Rams; was taken to heaven
      prematurely and then returned as Leo Farnsworth
      to buy the team; was killed by his wife, played by
      Dyan Cannon and his private secretary played by
      Charles Grodin; then returned as Tom Jarrett to
      score the winning touchdown in the SB game.
6.   Dick Enberg and Curt Gowdy.
7.   John Matuszak, who played for Oakland in SB XI
      and XV in the story about the North Dallas Bulls
      football team. Other SBers featured were Fred
      Biletnikoff, 49ers linebacker Dan Bunz, Rams
      tackle Doug France, Rams safety Jeff Severson,
      and 49ers defensive tackle Louie Kelcher (he was
      with the Chargers at the time he made the movie).
8.   *Busting*
9.   *The Longest Yard.*
10.   Fred Williamson.

MOVIES 2
Questions

1. Which ABC made-for-TV movie ran six days before SB XII, showing a plot by gamblers to fix the results of the game?
2. Which Denver running back had his life threatened after that movie?
3. Who scripted, co-produced, and starred in *Boss Nigger* about a bounty hunter?
4. Charlton Heston and John Cassavetes star, with Vikings QB Joe Kapp in a SB horror football flick with a sniper in the stadium. What's it's title?
5. Which Steelers running back was the subject of the 1980 movie *Fighting Back*?
6. Which 1973 movie was "Six times tougher than *Shaft*! Six times rougher than *Superfly*!" featuring Carl Eller, Gene Washington, Mercury Morris, Willie Lanier, and Mean Joe Greene?
7. Who was the Northwestern University architect student became an All-Big Ten flanker and later was in *Tell Me That You Love Me, Junie Moon*?
8. Who is the defensive end for the Rams (SB XIV) single-handedly battled terrorists in this 1987 good guys-bad guys flick?
9. Who played offense in high school and college, under the coaching of Ara Parseghian, and then played Spearchucker in the film *M*A*S*H*?
10. Who was the running back for the Vikings who was in *Dead Aim* and a more respectable 1991 flick called *Queen's Logic* with Kevin Bacon, Linda Fiorentino, John Malkovich, Joe Mantegna, Ken Olin, Tom Waits, and Jamie Lee Curtis?

MOVIES 2
Answers

1.   *Superdome,* shot for three months in the New Orleans Superdome.
2.   Jon Keyworth, causing security to screen his mail and guard him and his room. Commissioner Rozelle labeled the film as "ill-timed" and "in poor taste."
3.   Fred Williamson.
4.   It's the 1976 film *Two Minute Warning,* shot in Los Angeles Memorial Coliseum.
5.   Rocky Bleier. The movie starred Robert Urich, Art Carney, Bonnie Bedelia, Richard Herd, Howard Cosell, Steve Tannen, and Bubba Smith detailing how Bleier overcame near-crippling injuries suffered in Vietnam to go on as successful football player.
6.   *The Black Six.*
7.   Fred Williamson.
8.   Fred Dryer, also being seen at the time in the TV show *Hunter.*
9.   Fred Williamson.
10.   Ed Marinaro.

MVP 1
Questions

1. In SB XVI, there was a tie for MVP, the first time in SB history. Who received the MVP nods?
2. Who was the first player of a losing team to win the SB MVP award?
3. Bart Starr was the first player to win back-to-back MVP awards, in SB games I and II. Only one other player has matched that feat. Who is he?
4. The Pittsburgh Steelers won four SB games between 1975 and 1980, garnering four MVP titles for three of their players. Who were they?
5. Redskin John Riggins was voted MVP in which SB game? What record did he set?
6. This Kansas City Chiefs QB completed 12 of 17 attempts for 142 yards to make him the fourth QB to win MVP. Who is he?
7. What is the official title of the MVP award and when was it adopted?
8. The MVP award has gone to QBs in sixteen of the 30 games played. These 16 awards have gone to twelve different players. Who are they?
9. Although three teams have won four or more SB contests, only one of them has had six players named MVP. Which team and who are they?
10. Bart Starr and Terry Bradshaw have each won two MVP awards, one player has received three such honors. Who is he?

MVP 1
Answers

1. Randy White and Harvey Martin, Dallas Cowboys, for their tremendous pass rushing against the Denver Broncos.
2. Linebacker Chuck Howley, Dallas Cowboys, in SB V against the Baltimore Colts.
3. Terry Bradshaw, Steelers QB in Super Bowl games XIII and XIV.
4. Franco Harris (IX), Lynn Swann (X), and Terry Bradshaw (XIII and XIV)
5. SB XVII, against the Miami Dolphins when Riggo rushed for 166 yards.
6. Len Dawson, in the last Super Bowl before the leagues merged.
7. The Pete Rozzell Trophy, at SB XXV.
8. Bart Starr (I, II), Joe Namath (III), Len Dawson (IV), Roger Staubach (VI), Terry Bradshaw (XIII, XIV), Jim Plunkett (XV), Joe Montana (XVI, XIX, XXIV), Phil Simms (XXI), Doug Williams (XXII), Mark Rypien (XXVI), Troy Aikman (XXVII), and Steve Young (XXIX).
9. Dallas Cowboys, Chuck Howly, Roger Staubach, Harvey Martin, Troy Aikman and Emmitt Smith, and Larry Brown.
10. Former 49ers QB Joe Montana in SB XVI, XIX, and XXIV.

MVP 2
Questions

1.   Who is the only safety who has won the Super Bowl MVP award.
2.   Who won MVP for SB XXX?
3.   Who was the last defensive player to win the Super Bowl MVP?
4.   Who is the only MVP to wear the same jersey number as the game in which he played?
5.   Who was the first man to score three TDs in a SB game, who did not win a MVP nod?
6.   Which two players in SB XXIX were seeking their second MVP award?
7.   Of the 31 MVP awards presented in the first 30 games (Randy White and Harvey Martin shared the honor is SB XII), how many running backs have collected the trophy?
8.   Who are the three wide receivers to receive Super Bowl MVP honors?
9.   Has a kicker ever received the MVP prize in a SB game? If so, who?
10.   How many years passed between Joe Montana's first and last SB MVP prizes?

MVP 2
Answers

1. Jake Scott of the Miami Dolphins in SB VII, with two interceptions, including one in the end zone to kill a Redskins drive.
2. Dallas cornerback Larry Brown for picking off Neil O'Donnell twice.
3. Richard Dent, in SB XX when the Bears destroyed the Patriots.
4. Joe Montana, who was wearing 16 when the 49ers won SB XVI.
5. Roger Craig in Super Bowl XIX, when the award went to Montana.
6. Defensive end Richard Dent (XX) and wide receiver Jerry Rice (XXIII).
7. Six times (Larry Csonka, Franco Harris, John Riggins, Marcus Allen, Ottis Anderson, and Emmitt Smith).
8. Lynn Swann, Fred Biletnikoff, and Jerry Rice.
9. No.
10. Eight, between SB XVI and XXIV.

NICKNAMES 1
Question

1. Freddie Williamson, a cornerback for the Chiefs in SB I was known as:
    a) the bulldozer b) the hammer c) the chain saw
2. Which defensive team was called "Eleven Angry Men"?
3. Who was the Mad Bomber?
4. The 1974 Pittsburgh Steelers defensive line had what nickname?
5. The 1975 Dallas defensive squad carried what nickname?
6. The Killer Bees three-four defense met the Hogs offense in a SB rematch of teams from ten years earlier. What teams did the Killer Bees and the Hogs play for?
7. Why were they called the Killer Bees?
8. Who were the Hogs and who was the Boss Hog?
9. What nickname did Nick Buoniconti, Manny Fernandez, Dick Anderson, Jake Scott, Vern Den Herder, and Bob Matheson have from 1971 to 1974?
10. Who were the Mother Hens?

NICKNAMES 1
Answers

1. Freddie "the hammer" Williamson vowed to destroy the Vikings with his hammer blows, "A karate blow having great velocity and delivered perpendicular to the earth's latitude --- a lethal muthuh."
2. The Raiders defense in Super Bowl II.
3. Raider's QB, Daryl Lamonica who played in SB II
4. The Steel Curtain, with Joe Greene, Jack Ham, L.C. Greenwood, Ernie Holmes, Dwight White, Andy Russell, Jack Lambert, and Mel Blount.
5. The Doomsday Unit or Doomsday Defense, with Bob Lilly, George Andrie, Jethro Pugh, Willie Townes, Mel Renfro, Cornell Green, and Mike Gaechter.
6. The Killer Bees were the Dolphins and the Hogs played for the Redskins, in SB XVII which was a rematch of Super Bowl VII. The Dolphins won the first, the Redskins won the second.
7. Because each last name started with a B, Bob Baumhower, Doug Beters, Glenn Blackwood, Kim Bokamper, Lyle Blackwood and Bob Brudzinski.
8. The Redskins' Hogs, averaging 6'5" and 280 pounds, tackle to tackle were Joe Jacoby, Russ Grimm, Jeff Bostic, George Starke and Fred Dean and Mark May. Offensive Coach Joe Bugel was the Boss Hog.
9. They were the Miami Dolphins "No-Name Defense."
10. The offensive linemen who protected Joe Namath in the 1968, SB III season.

NICKNAMES 2
Questions

1.   Who was the "Mad Stork?"
2.   An easy one. Why is William Perry called the "Refrigerator"?
3.   Who were the Smurfs?
4.   Who were the Over the Hill Gang members?
5.   What is Max McGee's given first name?
6.   Who was known as Furnace Face, Whiskey Bill, and Billy the Kid?
7.   Why did Jamie Williams of the San Francisco 49ers like to be called Spiderman?
8.   What is Cincinnati QB Boomer Esiason's real name and why is he called Boomer?
9.   Who were Butch Cassidy and the Sundance Kid?
10.   Which team went to the SB XII behind the defensive prowess of the Orange Crush?

NICKNAMES 2
Answers

1.   Baltimore Colts (V) and Raiders (XI, XV, XVIII) linebacker Ted Hendricks, who was a slim, but tall 6'7."

2.   Because the former Chicago Bears, while officially clocked in at as much as 326, is said to have weighed much more, and was considered as big as a refrigerator.

3.   Alvin Garrett, Virgil Seay, Charlie Brown, members of the receiving team of the Washington Redskins from 1981 to 1984.

4.   The Washington Redskins of SB VII were the "Over the Hill Gang," a group of experienced pros including QB Billy Kilmer; and defensive aces Jack Pardee and Roosevelt Taylor.

5.   William M. McGee of the Green Bay Packers.

6.   Redskins Billy Kilmer.

7.   Williams read comic books to get psyched up by the heroes who were out to save the world or get the villain, so he could see himself doing that on the football field.

8.   Norman Julius Esiason, because from the time he was in utero he was kicking and "booming."

9.   Miami running backs Larry Csonka (Sundance) and Jim Kiick (Butch).

10.   Denver Broncos. In the process of compiling a 12-2 record, the city's fans developed an "Orange Crush" on their team.

NICKNAMES 3
Questions

1. Who was known as Freddie the Foot?
2. Of the SB participating teams, which team nickname comes first alphabetically?
3. Which San Francisco wide receiver is known as Skeets?
4. Who was called Ozark Ike, the Rifleman, and the Blond Bomber?
5. Who was Roger the Dodger?
6. Which wide receiver for the Dallas Cowboys was called Bambi?
7. How and when did Broadway Joe get his name?
8. What was Earl Lambeau's nickname and why?
9. What was John "Riggo" Riggins' nickname?
10. Who were the Purple People Eaters?

NICKNAMES 3
Answers

1. The Minnesota Vikings kicker, Fred Cox.
2. Chicago Bears.
3. Renaldo Nehemiah, who played on the 49ers victorious SB XIX team, by his father when he was just learning to crawl.
4. Steelers' Terry Bradshaw, who was born in Shreveport, LA although Shreveport is not in the Ozarks. The Blond Bomber was left over from college days. The Rifleman came from his bullet-intensity and direction-straight passes.
5. Dallas Cowboys QB Roger Staubach, because of his scrambling ability to dodge incoming defensive linemen--as in Dicken's character from *Oliver Twist*. The rhyming factor didn't hurt.
6. Lance Alworth, after the fleet-footed critter in the story of the same name. He could scamper, leap high, and make magic catches.
7. After appearing on the cover of a 1965 *Sports Illustrated* issue. His prowess on the field and his reputation with the ladies lit up Manhattan brighter than many Broadway shows.
8. "Curly," because his hair was. He started the Green Bay Packers, played for them, and coached them.
9. The Diesel, for his ability at 6'2" and 240 pounds to plow through the defense.
10. The Minnesota Vikings gigantic, ferocious-looking defensive line, dressed in their purple jerseys, were labeled that after the song of the same name.

NICKNAMES 4

Questions

1. Which Miami running back was known as the "Lawnmower"?
2. Other than being mean, how did Mean Joe Greene receive his nickname?
3. Who was Slug?
4. Who was The Snake?
5. Who gave Coach Wilbur Charles Ewbank his nickname of Weeb?
6. Which Miami Dolphin QB was known as Straight Arrow?
7. Who was Iron Mike?
8. Who was called Lassie?
9. How did Dallas Cowboys Thomas "Hollywood" Henderson get his nickname?
10. What is known as "The Drive"?

NICKNAMES 4
Answers

1.   Larry Csonka who'd lower his head on his 230-pound, 6'3" frame and mow down the opposing tackler.

2.   The Steelers defensive player's North Texas State defensive line was the Mean Green, from their antics and uniform color.

3.   Otis Taylor, wide receiver for the Kansas City Chiefs, who it's said slugged an opponent while playing for Prairie View A & M.

4.   Ken Stabler, QB for the Raiders. He received his nickname in high school football play.

5.   His younger brother who couldn't pronounce Wilbur.

6.   Bob Griese, for his quiet and shy ways.

7.   Former Chicago Bears head coach Mike Ditka.

8.   Jim O'Brien, who kicked the winning field goal with five seconds left between the Cowboys and the Baltimore Colts, in Super Bowl V because of his long hair.

9.   He gave it to himself, in acknowledgment of his showmanship.

10.   Joe Montana and the 49ers' 92-yard march through the former Joe Robbie Stadium in the last 3:10 of SB XXIII to defeat the Bengals 20-16.

ONLY
Questions

1. Who is the only player who has started on both offense and defense for SB games?
2. Who were the only two members of the 49ers SB XXIII team and the 49ers SB XVI ?
3. How many catches did veteran Steelers running back Rocky Bleier make in SB XIII?
4. Who was the only former Austin Peay State basketball player to catch a SB touchdown pass?
5. Which NFL team has only one side of the helmet with an insignia?
6. Who is the only man to play in a SB game and coach a SB winner?
7. Who is the only player to be in the World Series and a SB game?
8. SB XXIX was played on the 29th. Which is the only other time when the date and the game number matched?
9. Who is the only QB to be picked as a number one NFL draft choice during the 1980s who has not started in a SB?
10. Who's the only receiver to have two receptions in excess of 73 yards?

ONLY
Answers

1.   E. J. Holub, the Chiefs' starting right outside linebacker in Super Bowl I and their starting center in Super Bowl IV.
2.   QB Joe Montana and center Randy Cross.
3.   Only one, but it counted for seven yards, a touchdown, the lead, and eventually the win.
4.   Percy Howard for the Cowboys in SB X.
5.   Pittsburgh Steelers.
6.   "Iron Mike" Ditka played in SB VI for the Cowboys and coach the Bears in SB XX.
7.   Deion Sanders, cornerback for the 49ers in Super Bowl XXIX.
8.   SB XXVI, played on January 26 between the Redskins and the Bills.
9.   Vinny Testaverde.
10.   John Stallworth, for the Steelers in SB XIII and SB XIV.

OUTLAND TROPHY
Questions

1.   Who was the 1962 Outland winner who came out of Kansas City, was a linebacker for Kansas City in SB I and IV, was named to the Hall of Fame in 1983, and had his jersey number 78 retired?

2.   Who was the 1967 Outland winner who came out of USC, and played tackle for the Vikings in their four SB appearances, IV, VIII, IX, and XI?

3.   Who was the 1968 Outland Trophy winner who came out of Georgia and played for the Dolphins in SB VI, VII, and VIII?

4.   Who was the 1976 recipient of the Outland, and 1977 Maxwell Awards, out of Notre Dame, and was a defensive end for Cincinnati in SB XVI?

5.   Who was the 1980 Outland recipient out of Pittsburgh who was on the Hogs offensive line for the Redskins in SB VII, VIII, XXII?

6.   Who was the 1984 Outland victor who went on to play for the Bills and scored a safety against the Giants in SB XXV?

7.   Who was the 1986 Outland winner from Brigham Young who was a defensive tackle for the Bengals in SB XXIII and the Redskins in SB XXVI?

8.   Who was the 1990 Outland Trophy recipient nose tackle out of Miami-Florida who played for the Dallas Cowboys in SB XXVII and XXVIII?

9.   Who was the Utah State 1961 Outland winner who never played in a SB game, but was an NBC analyst for SB XIII, XV, XVII, XX, and XXIII?

10.   What is the origin of the Outland Trophy and who receives it?

OUTLAND TROPHY
Answers

1.   Bobby Bell.
2.   Ron Yary.
3.   Bill Stanfill.
4.   Ross Browner
5.   Mark May.
6.   Bruce Smith.
7.   Jason Buck.
8.   Russell Maryland.
9.   Merlin Olsen.
10.   The Outland Trophy is named for Dr. John Outland, a college All-American in the 1890s. It is awarded annually by the Football Writers Association of America to the outstanding interior lineman.

PASSES
Questions

1. What was the longest pass Joe Namath completed in his SB III victory over the Baltimore Colts?
2. In SB XIV, how many passes did Steelers' QB Bradshaw complete as he set two new SB records?
3. Four years later, in SB XIX, a new record was set by this QB who went 24 of 35 for 331 yards, with 3 TD passes and no interceptions and scoring on five straight series. Who was he?
4. Who holds the record for the most passes attempted in a SB career?
5. Who holds the record for the most passes attempted in a single SB game?
6. Who holds the record for the most passes completed in a single SB game?
7. Who holds the record for the highest completion percentage in a SB career, with a minimum of 40 attempts?
    a) Joe Montana b) Jim Plunkett c) Len Dawson
    d) Troy Aikman
8. Who passed for the longest completion?
9. Who was the first QB to pass for a 76 yard TD?
10. Who holds the record for the most passes intercepted in a SB career?

PASSES
Answers

1. Despite his flamboyant style, Namath went with a conservative game plan and the longest pass was 39 yards.
2. Bradshaw went 14 for 21 for 309 yards. He set the record for most career TD passes (nine) and the most career passing yards (932). He was named MVP for the second straight year.
3. 49ers QB Joe Montana, in defeating Miami 38-16
4. With 145 attempts, it's Jim Kelly, Buffalo, over four games.
5. Jim Kelly, with 58, in SB XXVI, against the Redskins.
6. Jim Kelly, with 31, when Buffalo lost to Dallas, in SB XXVIII.
7. d) Aikman with 71.9 percent, although the others listed are also high on that list.
8. Jim Plunkett and Doug Williams are tied, at 80 yards. Plunkett for Oakland against Philadelphia in SB XV and Williams in SB XXII against Denver. Each was good for a TD.
9. David Woodley in Miami's loss to Washington in SB XVII.
10. Craig Morton (Dallas and Denver), in two games, and Jim Kelly (Buffalo) in four games.

POINTS 1
Questions

1. How many points did the 49ers score in SB XXIX?
2. 49er Jerry Rice set a new career SB scoring record with 42 points in SB XXIX. Who held the record prior to that?
3. Ricky Watters and Jerry Rice each scored 18 points in SB XXIX, tying an existing SB record. Who held the record before that?
4. When Doug Brien scored seven PATs for SF in SB XXIX, he tied a SB record. Who held it?
5. SB XXIX set a record with a total of 75 points scored by San Francisco (49) and San Diego (26). What was the previous record?
6. Prior to SB XXIX when San Francisco (7) and San Diego (3) scored a record 10 PATs (including two 2-point conversions), which game(s) held the record for most PATs?
7. It's well-known that Doug Williams and the Redskins set a record for second quarter scoring with 35 in SB XXII. What's the record for first-quarter scoring and who holds it?
8. Two SB games have seen 21 points scored by both teams in the first quarter. Which are they?
9. When the 49ers scored seven PATs in SB XXIX, it tied the record with which two other teams?
10. What was unusual about the way the first points were scored in the first half of SB IX?

POINTS 1
Answers

1.   49.
2.   Franco Harris of Pittsburgh, Roger Craig and
     Jerry Rice of the 49ers, and Thurman Thomas of
     the Bills, with 24 points each.
3.   Roger Craig in SB XIX and Jerry Rice in XXIV,
     each playing for the 49ers.
4.   Mike Cofer, 49ers in XXIV, and Lin Elliott,
     Dallas in XXVII.
5.   SB XXVII, with a total of 69 points, with Dallas
     scoring 52 and Buffalo 17.
6.   Two games, SB XIII when Pittsburgh scored five
     and Dallas scored four; and SB XXVII when
     Dallas scored seven and Buffalo scored two.
7.   The record is 14 points in the first quarter shared
     by San Francisco in SB XXIX, Miami Dolphins
     in SB VIII, Oakland Raiders in SB XV, and
     Dallas Cowboys in SB XXVII.
8.   San Francisco (14) against San Diego (7) in SB
     XXIX and Dallas (14) against Buffalo (7) in SB
     XXVII.
9.   Itself in SB XXIV and Dallas in SB XXVII.
10. The Vikings were second down and eight at their
     own 10-yard line when they fumbled a handoff.
     The ball bounced backwards, Tarkenton fell on it,
     sliding into the end zone and Dwight White of the
     Pittsburgh Steelers downed him. The Steelers were
     awarded two points for a safety.

POINTS 2
Questions

1.   What was unusual about Terry Brown scoring for the Minnesota Vikings in SB IX?
2.   The SB IX game was noted for its low first-half score, 2-0 Steelers against the Vikings. What was the next lowest one-half score?
3.   Which was the lowest scoring SB game? What was the total point score of both teams? Which teams?
4.   Which is the next lowest?
5.   What was the lowest score for any team?
6.   What was the biggest margin a team overcame to win the Super Bowl?
7.   In the first SB game between the Green Bay Packers and the Kansas City Chiefs, two players scored rushing touchdowns. Who were they? (The other 24 points were scored on three passing touchdowns and a Kansas City field goal.)
8.   What was the narrowest margin of victory in a SB game?
9.   Which team has scored the most total points in SB games?
10.   Which team has scored the fewest total points in SB games?

POINTS 2
Answers

1.   Matt Blair broke through the Pittsburgh line to block Bobby Walden's punt and Viking Terry Brown, again of the defensive team, pounced on it in the end zone for six points.

2.   SB XXIII saw a 3-3 tie between the Cincinnati Bengals and the San Francisco 49ers.

3.   SB VII, Miami Dolphins (14) vs. Washington Redskins (7) for a total of 21 points.

4.   SB IX when the Pittsburgh Steelers defeated the Minnesota Vikings 16-6 for a total of 22 points.

5.   Miami Dolphins with 3 in SB VI, against the Dallas Cowboys (24).

6.   10 points, in SB XXII when Doug Williams quarterbacked the Washington Redskins to a 42-10 defeat over the Denver Broncos in the game with the 35-point second quarter.

7.   In the first half of SB I, Jim Taylor of the Packers scored on a 14-yard run. In the second half, Elijah Pitts scored two more rushing TDs for the Pack.

8.   One point, when the New York Giants defeated the Buffalo Bills 20-19 in SB XXV.

9.   Dallas Cowboys, with 221 points in eight games.

10.   The dubious honor is shared by the New England Patriots and the Philadelphia Eagles, with 10 points each, with each team in the SB once.

PUNTS 1
Questions

1. How many TDs have been scored on a punt return?
2. What was the longest run of a punt return and by whom?
    a) 45 yards b) 54 yards c) 39 yards d) 63 yards
3. What happened when the Vikings Matt Blair blocked Steelers Bobby Waldon's punt in the fourth quarter of SB IX?
4. What do Chris Mohr of the Bills and Kevin Butler of the Bears have in common?
5. What school did Giants punter Sean Landeta attend?
6. What school did Bengals punter (and wide receiver) Pat McInally attend?
7. What draft choice was Raiders' three-time Super Bowl punter Ray Guy of Mississippi State drafted in 1973?
8. What happened in SB X when the Steelers fumbled the punt snap from center, some four minutes into the first quarter?
9. What was the highest punting average in a game (with a minimum of four punts) in SB history?
10. What is the highest punting average in a Super Bowl career?

PUNTS 1
Answers

1. None.
2. a) 45 yards, by San francisco's John Taylor, who returned a punt 45 yards against the Cincinnati Bengals in SB XXIII.
3. The Vikings scored their only points, missing the extra point and losing 16-6.
4. Both participated in the Punt, Pass & Kick competition.
5. Towson State, in Maryland.
6. Harvard.
7. Raiders' Al Davis astounded the experts by using his first draft choice for the punter.
8. Dallas took over and Staubach threw to Drew Pearson for six points. It was the only time that season that Pittsburgh allowed a team to score in the first quarter. Steelers won 21-17.
9. Bryan Wagner of San Diego, in SB XXIX, with 48.8 yards.
10. Kansas City Chiefs' Jerrel Wilson, with ten punts in two games, with an average of 46.5 yards

PUNTS 2
Question

1.   Who holds the record for most total Super Bowl punt returns?
2.   Who holds the record for the most total SB punt returns in a single game?
3.   What distinction does Miami's Jake Scott have?
4.   What record does Oakland/Vikings punter Mike Eischeid hold?
5.   Lee Johnson, Bengals punter, holds the SB record for the longest punt? How long was it?
6.   Who has the record for the most punts in a single Super Bowl game?
7.   Who was the first player to return five punts in a single Super Bowl game?
8.   Who was the first player to have three fair catches from punts in a single Super Bowl game?
9.   Who holds the record for the most yards gained from punt returns, in a SB career?
10. Who holds the record for the most yards gained from punt returns, in a single game?

PUNTS 2
Answers

1.   Willie Wood, Green Bay Packers, Theo Bell of Pittsburgh Steelers, and John Taylor of the San Francisco 49ers, each with six in two games.
2.   Mike Nelms, of the Washington Redskins, with six in SB XVII, against losing Miami.
3.   The MVP from SB VII, holds the record for six SB punt returns, over three games.
4.   He has the most punts in SB career, with 17, in three games.
5.   63 yards, against San Francisco in SB XXIII, besting the Patriot's Rich Camarillo's record of 62 yards, set against Chicago in SB XX.
6.   Ron Widby, of Dallas with nine, in their losing effort to Baltimore in SB V.
7.   Willie Wood, of Green Bay against Oakland in SB II. That was tied by Dana McLemore, of San Francisco, against Miami in SB XIX.
8.   Ron Gardin, Baltimore against Dallas in SB V.
9.   John Taylor, from San Francisco, with 94 yards over two games.
10. John Taylor, San Francisco, with 56 yards, against Cincinnati in SB XXIII.

QUARTERBACK 1
Questions

1.   Which four-time SB QB was called dumb while playing for the NFL?
2.   When Joe Namath was signed to the New York Jets for the lofty sum of $400,000 or so, how much was the average NFL pro QB receiving?
      a) $10,000, b) $40,000, c) $100,000 d) $200,000
3.   In the famed SB III, Namath said there were five quarterbacks in the AFL who were better than the Colt's Earl Morrall. Who were they?
4.   Where was Namath when he guaranteed the Jets would defeat the Colts in SB III?
5.   1986 Hall of Fame inductee, and Georgia graduate Fran Tarkenton started how many games as SB QB for the Minnesota Vikings?
6.   What do quarterbacks Steve Young, Boomer Esiason, and Ken Stabler have in common?
7.   Which Stanford Heisman Trophy winner went on to QB a team to two SB victories?
8.   Terry Bradshaw attended Louisiana Tech. Did he graduate?
9.   What do quarterbacks Bart Starr, Fran Tarkenton, Phil Simms, John Unitas, Len Dawson, Bob Griese, and Joe Namath have in common?
10.   What was Phil Simms pass completion record in SB XXI against the Denver Broncos?

QUARTERBACK 1
Answers

1. Terry Bradshaw, who led the Pittsburgh Steelers to victories in Super Bowls IX, X, XIII, and XIV.
2. b) Namath's lofty salary was ten times that of the established NFL quarterback, which averaged about $40,000.
3. Daryle Lamonica of the Oakland Raiders, John Hall of the Chargers, Bob Griese of the Dolphins, Babe Parilli (the number two but ancient QB) of the Jets, and Joe Willie Namath.
4. At the Miami Touchdown Club annual banquet, where he was being honored as the Outstanding Player of the Year. "We will win Sunday. I guarantee you."
5. Three, in VIII, IX, and XI, all losing efforts.
6. All are left-handed.
7. Jim Plunkett, receiving the award in 1970, went on to QB the Oakland and L.A. Raiders to Super Bowls XV and XVIII.
8. Yes, in 1970, with a B.S. in Liberal Arts.
9. Their football jersey numbers have been retired. Starr, 15 Packers; Tarkenton, 10 Vikings; Simms, 11 Giants; Unitas, 19 Colts; Dawson, 16 Chiefs; Griese, 12 Dolphins; and Namath, 12 Jets.
10. Simms completed an amazing 22 of 25 pass attempts in the 39-20 victory.

QUARTERBACK 2
Questions

1. Which record-setting SB QB went on the coaching staff for the United States Naval Academy?
2. What do Jeff Hostetler, Doug Williams, and Jim Plunkett have in common.
3. How many interceptions did Joe Montana have in four Super bowl games?
4. How many SB MVP awards did Joe Montana win in his four 49ers appearances?
5. Who was the 82nd player picked in the 1979 NFL draft?
6. Which quarterbacks wore the same jersey number as the SB they played in?
7. Which QB is the only one to wear the same jersey number as SB game AND win the MVP award?
8. What do Oakland Raiders QB Ken Stabler, Jets QB Joe Namath and Green Bay QB Bart Starr have in common?
9. Who replaced Roger Staubach as QB for the Dallas Cowboys?
10. Who was the first QB to score a SB touchdown?

QUARTERBACK 2
Answers

1.   Redskins' Doug Williams, who was responsible for the mind-numbing 35-point second quarter against the Denver Broncos in SB XXII.
2.   All had been around for years as backup or journeymen quarterbacks before coming into Super Bowl fame.
3.   None.
4.   Three, the fourth went to wide receiver Jerry Rice.
5.   Joe Montana.
6.   Roger Staubach, wore 12 and was in SB XII; Joe Montana, wore 16 and was in SB XVI; David Humm with the Raiders wore number 11 and was in SB XI.
7.   Joe Montana.
8.   They were all quarterbacks at Alabama prior to their pro careers. Additionally, Namath and Stabler each wore number 12 on their pro uniform.
9.   Danny White.
10.   Minnesota Vikings' Fran Tarkenton in SB VIII.

QUARTERBACK 3
Question

1. Which of these QBs led Dallas to their first Super
    Bowl victory?
    a) Steve Beuerlein b)Danny White   c) Roger
    Staubach   d) Craig Morton
2. Who were the two QBs in SB XII between Dallas
    and Denver?
3. Which QBs led Oakland to is first SB win?
    a) Daryle Lamonica   b) Jim Plunkett c) David
    Humm d) Ken Stabler
4. Which Redskin was QB for the team's first SB
    victory?
    a) Billy Kilmer b) Joe Theismann c) Sonny
    Jurgeson d) Doug Williams
5. Who was the NFL quarterback on Richard
    Nixon's enemies list?
6. Which team originally drafted quarterback Joe
    Theismann?
7. His jersey, number 11, was retired by the Giants
    on Monday September 4, 1995. What pick of the
    Giants was this Morehead State QB selected in
    the 1979 NFL draft? What is his name?
8. Who was the first to QB four winning SB games?
9. Which one QB has led his teams to the Rose
    Bowl, the Canadian Football League title game,
    and the Super Bowl?
10. What field of study was Nebraska graduate and
    Rams QB Vince Ferragamo following?

QUARTERBACK 3
Answers

1. c) Staubach, in SB VI. Morton was at the helm the previous year when the Cowboys lost to Baltimore.
2. Staubach for Dallas; Morton for Denver.
3. d) Stabler, in SB XI. Lamonica was QB in their first effort, in SB II.
4. b) Theismann, in SB XVII against the Dolphins, ten years after Kilmer had struggled in vain against the season-perfect Dolphins in SB VII.
5. Jets quarterback Joe Namath.
6. Miami Dolphins.
7. Phil Simms was the Giants number one pick.
8. Terry Bradshaw, Pittsburgh Steelers.
9. Joe Kapp, leading California in the Rose Bowl, British Columbia in the Grey Cup, and Minnesota Vikings in Super Bowl IV.
10. Number 15 was a medical student.

QUARTERBACK 4
Questions

1. Which QB was a No. 1 Prep QB in America, minor league baseball player for one summer in the Yankees organization, two-time All-American QB for Stanford, owner of five NCAA Division I-A records and nine major Pac-10 records, and son of a successful football coach?
2. Which QB was great at sports and also valedictorian at his high school class?
3. How many of the Super Bowl MVP awards have gone to QBs?
4. Which QB gave new meaning to the New Orleans name "Crescent City"?
5. Which QB threw for the most TDs in a single Super Bowl game?
    a) Joe Montana b) Terry Bradshaw c) Doug Williams d) Steve Young
6. Joe Namath spent 11 years leading the New York Jets. With which team did he end his career?
7. San Francisco and Cincinnati played each other in the SB twice. Name the starting quarterbacks.
8. Name the winning QB in each of the first four Super Bowls.
9. The Redskins have been to the SB five times with four different QBs. Who are they?
10. Gale Gilbert, San Diego Chargers back-up QB in SB XXIX is distinguished in which way?

QUARTERBACK 4
Answers

1.   Denver Broncos' quarterback John Elway.
2.   Giants QB Jeff Hostetler.
3.   Seventeen.
4.   Bears' quarterback Jim McMahon mooned a helicopter during a team practice.
5.   d) Steve Young, with six, in SB XXIX. Montana threw for five, the other three threw for four each.
6.   Los Angeles Rams.
7.   Joe Montana each time for San Francisco; Kenny Anderson and Boomer Esiason for Cincinnati.
8.   Bart Starr of Green Bay, I & II; Joe Namath of New York Jets, III; and Len Dawson of Kansas City, Super Bowl IV.
9.   Billy Kilmer, VII; Joe Theismann, XVII and XVII; Doug Williams, XXII; and Mark Rypien, XXVI.
10.   As a member of the Buffalo Bills and San Diego Chargers, his teams were in five consecutive losing games. He didn't play for the first Bills game, he was inactive in the next three. Only in SB XXIX did he play, and he completed 3 of 6 passes for 30 yards and had one pass intercepted, in relief for Stan Humphries.

RECEIVERS 1
Questions

1. Which member of the Oakland Raiders caught four passes for 79 yards and took the MVP honor in SB XI?
2. When Terry Bradshaw threw that miracle 64-yard TD play in SB X, who caught the pass?
3. Why didn't Bradshaw see the completion?
4. Four years later, in SB IV, Bradshaw threw still another miracle pass, this one for a 73-yard touchdown play to defeat the Rams. Who caught this pass?
5. Joe Montana threw a last minute pass to win SB XXIII for the 49ers. Who caught it?
6. What, among other things, most distinguishes wide receiver Dwight Clark of the 49ers from the rest of the crowd?
7. San Francisco 49ers Jerry Rice holds the records for the most yards gained with 512 in three SB games. Whose record did he break?
8. In SB IX, between Pittsburgh Steelers and Minnesota Vikings, how many passes did Lynn Swann catch?
9. Which receiver trains in the off season by running up the hills of San Francisco?
    a) Shawn Jefferson b) Alvin Harper c) Jerry Rice d) James Loftus
10. Who was the only former Austin Peay State basketball player to catch a SB touchdown pass?

RECEIVERS 1
Answers

1.   Fred Biletnikoff, wide receiver for the Raiders, made four key receptions in the Raiders 32-14 defeat over the Minnesota Vikings.
2.   Wide receiver Lynn Swann.
3.   Because he'd been knocked unconscious on the play.
4.   John Stallworth.
5.   John Taylor, primarily because the Cincinnati defense was keying in on Jerry Rice.
6.   He's the only wide receiver to have played in a SB game to have his jersey number, 87, retired.
7.   Pittsburgh Steelers' Lynn Swann, who had 364 yards in four games. After him is Andre Reed, Buffalo Bills, with 323 yards in four games.
8.   None.
9.   c) San Francisco 49ers' Jerry Rice.
10. Percy Howard for the Cowboys in SB X, his first and last reception, against the Steelers.

RELATIVES
Questions

1. This defensive tackle played for the Bears and the Bills, but he went to SB VI as a Dolphin; his son, a guard/center played for the Chargers, but went to SB XXVII and XXVIII as a Cowboy. Who are these father and son players?

2. This Hall of Fame guard from Alabama played for the Patriots in SB XX and his brother played for the Raiders' SB XVIII team. Who are they?

3. Which brothers were safeties on the Dolphins Killer Bees squad for SB XVII and XIX?

4. One brother was a linebacker for the 49ers in SB XXIII and the other was a tackle for the 49ers in SB XVI and XIX. Their names?

5. Who were the running back and cornerback brothers on the Bengals SB XVI team?

6. From Iowa City came a linebacker for the Vikings for SB IV, VIII, IX and XI and a center for the Bears in SB XX. What are their names?

7. Who are the center who played for the Patriots in SB XX and his brother, a tackle for the Chargers in XXIX?

8. Who are the brothers who played wide receiver for the Raiders in SB XVIII and running back for the Eagles in SB XV?

9. Which brothers played for the Steelers (linebacker) of SB IX, X, XIII, and XIV and the Dolphins (guard) SB XVII and XIX?

10. Which brother kicked for the Steelers in SB XIV and the Giants in SB XXV, while the other kicked for the Raiders in SB XV and XVIII?

RELATIVES
Answers

1. Frank and Frank Cornish.
2. John and Charley Hannah, whose dad, Herb, was a tackle for the New York Giants, in the days before SB games.
3. Glenn Blackwood and Lyle Blackwood, both veteran safeties, for Miami in SB XVII and XIX, the first brothers to line up together for a Super Bowl game.
4. Jim and Keith Fahnhorst.
5. Archie and Ray Griffin.
6. Wally (Vikings) and Jay (Bears) Hilgenberg.
7. Pete (Patriots) and Stan (Chargers) Brock.
8. Cle (Raiders) and Wilbert (Eagles) Montgomery.
9. Loren (Steelers) and Jeff (Dolphins) Toews.
10. Chris (Raiders) and Matt (Steelers and Giants) Bahr.

RETIRED NUMBERS
Questions

1.   Which SB team has retired the most uniform numbers in the NFL?

2.   Has any SB player had his number retired by more than one team?

3.   Who's the only kicker to have his number retired by the Kansas City Chiefs?

4.   Which two SB quarterbacks wore number 12 and have had their jersey number retired?

5.   Who is the only SB flanker to have his number retired?

6.   Who is the only wide receiver to have played in a SB game to have his jersey number retired?

7.   How many jersey numbers have the Cowboys retired?

8.   Who is the only SB guard to have his number retired?

9.   Who was the 1962 Outland Trophy winner who came out of Kansas City, was a swift linebacker for Minnesota in SB I and II, was named to the Hall of Fame in 1983, and had his jersey number 78 retired?

10.   How many jersey numbers have the Steelers retired?

RETIRED NUMBERS
Answers

1.   The Bears, with 13.
2.   No.
3.   Jan Stenerud, 3, is the only placekicker to be named to the Hall of Fame.
4.   Dolphins quarterback Bob Griese and Jets quarterback Joe Namath.
5.   Don Maynard, number 13, New York Jets.
6.   Dwight Clark of the 49ers, number 87.
7.   None, but they do have a Ring of Honor at Texas Stadium which includes nine players Tony Dorsett, Chuck Howley, Lee Roy Jordan, Bob Lilly, Don Meredith, Don Perkins, Mel Renfro, Roger Staubach and Randy White -- and one coach, Tom Landry.
8.   John Hannah of the Patriots, wearing jersey number 73.
9.   Bobby Bell.
10.   None.

RIVALRIES
Questions

1. The Baylor-TCU rivalry has gone on for more than 100 years with no overall dominance. Are there more SB players from Baylor or TCU?
2. The Harvard-Yale rivalry is even longer, with Yale dominating. How about SB players?
3. How about the Princeton-Yale competition with Yale dominating on a three-to-two average. Does Yale or Princeton lead with SB players?
4. The granddaddy of all college rivalries is between Lafayette and Lehigh, with Lafayette clearly ahead. How about in SB games?
5. Texas-Texas A&M has had a great rivalry with Texas in dominance. And their SB records?
6. The UCLA-USC rivalry has seen USC come out on top many more times than UCLA. Does either stand ahead of the other in SB players?
7. For a great rivalry, head for Notre Dame and Purdue country, where Notre Dame has about a two-to-one lead. How about in SB games?
8. Regarding the three military service academies, Army and Navy are neck-and-neck, with the Air Force beating both Army and Navy in more than two dozen years of battles. And in SB players?
9. In the Minnesota-Wisconsin rivalry, Minnesota's has a strong dominance. What about their SB records?
10. Down south, at Georgia-Georgia Tech, Georgia leads almost three-to-two in about nine decades of battles. How do they do on the SB field?

RIVALRIES
Answers

1.   Baylor leads almost 2-1, with 17 players vs. ten.
2.   Yale triumphs again, with a majority of five-to-two SB players.
3.   Again, it's Yale, with their five to Princeton's two.
4.   Lehigh wins this one, with one; Lafayette has had none.
5.   Texas is only slightly ahead, 19-17.
6.   It's almost a tie with USC nosing out UCLA by 38-37. However, five UCLA QBs have gone to SB games, while on three from USC have.
7.   It's a runaway for Notre Dame with 32 players to Purdue's 7.
8.   It's an easy win for Navy with two (Roger Staubach and Phil McConkey), one for Air Force (Chad Hennings) and none for Army.
9.   Again, it's Minnesota with 21 and Wisconsin with 10.
10.   Georgia's dominance is not quite as strong, but it's still two-to-one with 16 for Georgia and eight for Tech.

SAFETIES 1
Questions

1. What's the most number of safeties scored in a single SB game?
    a) 1   b) 2   c) 3   d) 4
2. Which SB game saw the first safety scored?
3. How long was it before another SB game saw a safety scored?
4. Which SB game was the last to have a safety scored?
5. Which team has scored the most safeties in all SB history?
    a) Dallas   b) Pittsburgh   c) Buffalo   d) Washington
6. How many times has a safety been scored in Super Bowl history?
7. Which team has scored a safety and had one scored against them?
    a) Pittsburgh   b) Dallas   c) Buffalo   d) New York Giants
8. In SB XXV, who did Bills Bruce Smith tackle for their second-period safety?
9. Who did Chicago's defensive end Henry Waechter tackle in their defeat of the Patriots in SB XX for a fourth-period safety?
10. Which Redskins safety was known for his whistling bird calls?

SAFETIES 1
Answers

1.   One.
2.   SB IX Steelers vs. Vikings.
3.   One year, to SB X, Steelers vs. Cowboys.
4.   SB XXV, Bills vs. Giants.
5.   Pittsburgh, with two, against Minnesota in IX and Dallas in SB X.
6.   Five, by Reggie Harrison (Pittsburgh against Dallas, SB X), Henry Waechter (Chicago vs New England, XX), George Martin (New York Giants against Denver, XXI), and Bruce Smith (Buffalo vs New York Giants XXV).
7.   Giants, against Denver, Super Bowl XXI, and by Buffalo in Super Bowl XXV.
8.   Giants Quarterback Jeff Hostetler
9.   Waechter nailed back-up quarterback Steve Grogan after first-string quarterback Tony Eason was pulled.
10.   Mike Nelms, who professionally was known as a punt-return specialist.

SAFETIES 2
Questions

1.   Who's the only safety to be awarded MVP
      honors?
2.   Which two safeties have played for two SB teams.
3.   Which two brothers were safeties and what team
      did they play for?
4.   Who are the four safeties who have worn the same
      number on their jersey as the SB game in which
      they played.
5.   Who are the two safeties to play in SB games who
      came out of Yale?
6.   Who was the first player to record a safety in SB
      history?
7.   Who scored the only points in the second period
      of SB XXI between the Giants and the Broncos?
8.   Although Pittsburgh scored 14 points in the fourth
      quarter of SB X, two of those points were from a
      safety. Who scored it?
9.   Has there ever been a scoreless SB half?
10.   Who are the two safeties who have each been in
      five Super Bowl games?

SAFETIES 2
Answers

1. Jake Scott, Miami Dolphins, in SB VII, for his two interceptions, including one in the end zone to kill a Redskins' drive, and some excellent punt returns.

2. Dave Duerson for the Bears (XX) and Giants (XXV); and Kenny Hill for the Raiders (XVIII) and Giants (XXI).

3. Glenn Blackwood and Lyle Blackwood, both veteran safeties, for Miami in SB XVII, XIX.

4. Tony Lilly, Broncos, #22; Danny Copeland, Redskins, #26; Thomas Everett, Cowboys, #27; Darren Woodson, Cowboys, #28.

5. Kenny Hill who played for the LA Raiders and Gary Fencik who played for the Bears.

6. Dwight White, Pittsburgh Steelers, SB IX, after downing Fran Tarkenton's fumbled pass attempt in the second quarter of SB IX, resulting in the first points scored in the game.

7. Giants defensive end George Martin, when he sacked Broncos QB Elway in the end zone for a safety.

8. The Steelers' Reggie Harrison blocked the Cowboys' Mitch Hoopes' punt through the end zone.

9. No, but it came close. In SB IX it was 7:49 into the second quarter before Steelers' Dwight White tackled Vikings QB Fran Tarkenton in the end zone for a safety.

10. Cliff Harris and Charlie Waters each played 5 SB games wearing the Cowboys uniform in SB V, VI, X, XII, XIII.

STADIA 1
Questions

1.   Where was the first "Super Bowl" played?
2.   Where and when was the first indoor SB game played?
3.   Which stadia have been home to the most SB games?
4.   Prior to playing at the Louisiana Superdome, three SB games were played in New Orleans. Which field was used?
5.   Two states have had nine SB games. Which state has had the most different venues for SB games and what are they?
6.   Since 1989, the games in Miami have been played at the former Joe Robbie Stadium. Where were the SB games played in Miami before that?
7.   SB XXVII was played in Pasadena. Where was it originally scheduled to be played and why was the venue changed?
8.   Where was the first cold-weather city to hold a super bowl, what year, and which Super Bowl?
9.   Which two stadia have been home to a SB game and the World Series?
10. Thirteen stadia have been home to SB games. Which are they?

STADIA 1
Answers

1.   Memorial Coliseum, Los Angeles, 1/15/67.
2.   Louisiana Superdome, New Orleans, SB XII.
3.   The Rose and Orange Bowls, with five each.
4.   Tulane Stadium.
5.   California, two in Memorial Coliseum, five in Pasadena's Rose Bowl, and one each in Jack Murphy Stadium, and Stanford Stadium.
6.   The Orange Bowl.
7.   It was set for Phoenix, AZ, but changed because the state had vetoed a holiday honoring Martin Luther King, Jr's birthday.
8.   Pontiac Silverdome, SB XVI, Detroit, Michigan.
9.   Jack Murphy Stadium, for SB XXII and the Padres home games for the 1984 Fall Classic, and LA Memorial Coliseum, where SB I was played in 1967 and where the Dodgers played their home games in the 1959 World Series.
10.   Memorial Coliseum, LA; Orange Bowl, Miami; Tulane Stadium, New Orleans; Rice Stadium, Houston; Rose Bowl, Pasadena; Louisiana Superdome, New Orleans; Pontiac Silverdome, Pontiac, MI; Tampa Stadium, Tampa; Stanford Stadium, Palo Alto, CA; Jack Murphy Stadium, San Diego; the former Joe Robbie Stadium, Miami; Hubert H. Humphrey Metrodome, Minneapolis, MN; Georgia Dome, Atlanta, GA.

STADIA 2
Questions

1.   Of the seven games played in Miami, the Cowboys have appeared in two at the Orange Bowl and once at the former Joe Robbie. What is their record for those three games?
2.   The Baltimore Colts played two games in Miami. What is their record?
3.   In XXIII and XXIX the 49ers played in Miami, once at the Orange Bowl and once at the former Joe Robbie Stadium. What is their record?
4.   Five games have been played at the Rose Bowl. Has any team played there more than once?
5.   Which is the only stadium to be the SB venue for two consecutive games?
6.   Has any team ever played in its home field for a SB game?
7.   In which stadium was Joe Namath's SB victory prediction game played?
8.   Which two teams met in the first indoor stadium Super Bowl?
9.   What is the name of the stadium where SB XXX was played?
10.   How many SB games have been played in Houston's Astrodome?

STADIA 2
Answers

1.   They lost all three. In SB V against the Colts, in
      X and XIII, against the Steelers.
2.   They lost one to the Jets in III and defeated the
      Cowboys in V.
3.   They won both times.
4.   No. Ten different teams have appeared at the
      Rose Bowl. XI Raiders vs. Vikings; XIV Steelers
      vs. LA Rams; XVII Redskins vs. Dolphins; XXI
      Giants vs. Broncos; XXVII Cowboys vs Bills.
5.   Miami's Orange Bowl in Super Bowls II and III.
6.   No. The closest thing to home field advantage was
      when the Los Angeles Rams played the Pittsburgh
      Steelers in SB XIV in Pasadena. Home field didn't
      help much as LA lost 31-19. The next closest was
      San Francisco at Stanford defeating Cincinnati in
      SB XIX
7.   The Orange Bowl, Miami.
8.   The Cowboys and the Broncos in SB XII, in New
      Orleans.
9.   Sun Devil Stadium, Tempe, AZ.
10.   None.

TDs
Questions

1. Who scored the most TDs in a single game?
2. Who scored the most TDs in a personal Super Bowl history?
3. Who scored the first points, a TD, for the defense in a Super Bowl game?
4. Who scored the most TD passes in a personal Super Bowl career?
5. Who threw for the most TDs in a single SB game?
6. How many TDs have been scored after a fumble recovery in all 30 SB games?
    a) 2   b) 5   c) 7   d) 12
7. Which SB game had the most fumble recoveries leading to TDs?
8. Who recovered the other fumbles for TDs?
9. How many interceptions have resulted in TDs?
10. How many TDs have been scored from kick-off returns?

TDs
Answers

1.   49er's Ricky Watters, with three against San Diego, with two pass receptions and one run, in SB XXIX.
2.   Jerry Rice, in three games for San Francisco 49ers.
3.   Herb Adderly of Green Bay returned an interception 60 yards for a TD in SB II.
4.   Former 49ers QB Joe Montana, with 11 in four SB games.
5.   Steve Young, with six, for San Francisco, in Super Bowl XXIX.
6.   Five.
7.   SB XXVII, with Buffalo fumbling for two TDs. Jimmie Jones and Ken Norton each recovered a fumble that resulted in a TD.
8.   Mike Bass (Redskins against Dolphins), Mike Hegman (Dallas vs Pittsburgh), and James Washington (Dallas vs Buffalo in SB XXVIII).
9.   Four, by Green Bay against Oakland in SB II, Oakland against Minnesota in SB XI, by LA Raiders against Washington in SB XVIII, and by Chicago against New England in SB XX.
10.   Three, by Miami against Washington in SB XVII, by Cincinnati against San Francisco in SB XXII, and by San Diego against San Francisco in XXIX.

TELEVISION
Questions

1. Which television network covered SB I?
2. Which quarterback has thrown a football into a moving cab on the David Letterman Show and ridden a unicycle on the Conan O'Brien show?
3. On what TV soap opera did New York Giants linebacker Harry Carson make a 1979 appearance?
4. On what TV show did Rams defensive end Fred Dryer have a Magnum named Simon with which he would say to the bad guys "Simon says"?
5. By SB II, the game belonged to CBS, which had 12 cameras, with one in the Goodyear Blimp, and 4 video tape machines for slow motion (Slo-mo) replay, a 1963 invention developed by CBS director Tony Verna. How many cameras did CBS have for SB XIV?
    a) 12   b) 18   c) 23   d) 31
6. How much equipment did ABC use for the SB XXIX coverage?
7. Which Baltimore Colts defensive end spent a season as a night manager at a convenience store in the one-season ABC sitcom *Open All Night*?
8. To whom did the Raiders dedicate SB XV?
9. Which quarterback was featured in an April, 1996 episode of *Lois & Clark: The New Adventures of Superman*, written by Teri Hatcher?
10. Which Kansas City cornerback played Joe Pesci's boss in the short-lived TV show *Half Nelson*?

TELEVISION
Answers

1.   Both NBC and CBS covered the game, for CBS had been airing the NFL games and NBC the AFL games. Pat Summerall, Frank Gifford, and Jack Whitaker were the announcers for CBS; Curt Gowdy and Paul Christman for NBC.

2.   49ers Steve Young, after winning SB XXIX.

3.   One Life to Live.

4.   Dryer played Det. Sgt. Rick Hunter on the show called *Hunter*, which ran on NBC from 1984 through 1991.

5.   d) 31 cameras.

6.   ABC used 105,600 feet of camera and microphone wire, 200 crew members, 50 microphones, 27 cameras, 20 videotape machines, 11 announcers and 2 blimps with cameras.

7.   Charles "Bubba" Smith played Robin in this series with George Dzundza and Susan Tyrell. Smith then went on to appear in *Blue Thunder* and *Half Nelson* with Dick Butkus, and *Semi-Tough*.

8.   The recently-freed 52 American hostages, many of whom were comfortably ensconced at West Point, watching the festivities on wide-screen TV, festivities they most likely had missed the previous year.

9.   San Francisco 49ers Steve Young.

10.   Fred Williamson. The show ran from March 24 to May 10 of 1985.

TIME 1
Questions

1. How much time was left on the clock when Joe Montana found John Taylor in the end zone in SB XXIII to defeat the Cincinnati Bengals 20-16?
2. How much time was Miami's offense on the field in SB VI?
3. How much time was the Bills offense on the field in SB XXV?
4. In Buffalo's loss to the New York Giants in SB XXV, how much time was left before Buffalo converted a third-down play?
5. What happened in SB V with five seconds left on the clock?
6. How far into SB VII were the Redskins before they scored their first TD?
7. In SB XIII, what time period elapsed between two fourth-period TDs scored by the Steelers?
8. How much time was left in the first half of SB XV when Jim Plunkett threw the longest play in SB history, 80 yards, to Kenny King?
9. How many seconds remained in SB XVI when Bengals QB Ken Anderson scored on a three-yard pass to Dan Ross to almost make an historic comeback from a 20-0 49ers half-time lead?
10. Who kicked two field goals thirteen seconds apart for the San Francisco 49ers in SB XVI?

TIME 1
Answers

1.   34 seconds.
2.   20 minutes of the 60 in facing the Cowboys defense and losing to the Cowboys 24-3.
3.   A record-setting 19 minutes and 27 seconds, against the New York Giants, losing 20-19.
4.   Less than two minutes, the first team to earn this dubious honor.
5.   Rookie kicker Jim O'Brien kicked a 32-yard field goal to take the Baltimore Colts to a 16-13 victory over the Cowboys.
6.   There was 7:07 left in the game clock before they scored their one and only TD in losing to the season-long unbeatable Dolphins 14-7, and that only resulted from a misplayed field goal attempt and a fumble.
7.   19 seconds in defeating the Cowboys 35-31. Franco Harris had gone 22 yards up the middle to put Pittsburgh in front 28-17 when Randy White fumbled the kickoff and Dennis Winston recovered for the Steelers. Bradshaw hit Lynn Swann for an 18-yard TD pass on the first down.
8.   Nine seconds. Doug Williams and Ricky Sanders would duplicate that 80-yard record at SB XXII.
9.   16 seconds. Ross set a SB record with 11 receptions for 104 yards.
10.   San Francisco's Ray Wersching, in SB XVI, in defeating the Cincinnati Bengals 26-21.

TIME 2
Questions

1. How long did Joe Montana take to make "The Drive," the 92-yard TD march at the former Joe Robbie Stadium in SB XXIII?

2. Lynn Swann was the MVP of Super Bowl X after a 59-yard pass and five-yard run TD led the Steelers to a 21-17 defeat of the Cowboys. How much time was left in the game when he made this daring catch?

3. Rocky Bleier sealed the Pittsburgh victory over the Cowboys in SB XIII when he recovered an onside kick with how much time left on the clock?

4. How much time elapsed between the Cowboys' first and second TDs in the first quarter of SB XXVII against the Buffalo Bills?

5. How much time elapsed between the Cowboy's third and fourth TDs in the second quarter of SB XXVII?

6. How much time remained in the first half in SB XVIII when Raiders linebacker Jack Squirek intercepted Theismann deep in his territory for a TD and a dominating 21-3 halftime?

7. How much time had elapsed in the first period of SB XX before the first score?

8. How much time elapsed over the five scores the Redskins made in the second quarter of SB XXII?

9. How much time remained in SB XXV between the Giants and the Bills when Scott Norwood's 47-yard field-goal attempt went off its mark?

10. How much time had elapsed in SB XXIX before San Francisco made its first score?

TIME 2
Answers

1.   Montana's 49ers defeated the Bengals 20-16 in the last 3:10 of the game.
2.   3:02. Swan set a record with his 161 yards on four receptions.
3.   1 second.
4.   15 seconds.
5.   18 seconds.
6.   Seven seconds.
7.   1:19 when New England's Tony Franklin kicked a 36-yard field goal. They'd lose to Chicago 46-10.
8.   A paltry 5:47 for the five TDs in 18 plays.
9.   Four seconds.
10.   84 seconds, when Jerry Rice hauled in a long pass for a 44-yard TD.

UNIFORMS
Questions

1. Why were the Kansas City Chiefs players given Mickey Mouse ears by Coach Hank Stram just before SB I?
2. Which two NFL teams have helmets on their helmets?
3. Which professional football team was the first to put emblems on their helmets?
4. How many SB teams have animals or representations of animals on their helmets?
5. Which 4-time SB-losing club was derided for the striped socks in their original uniform?
6. On which eye does the Raiders' helmet warrior wear the patch?
7. Which team has retired the most uniform numbers?
8. Why did Kansas City Chiefs wear a red and blue AFL 10 patch on their uniforms for SB IV?
9. Before its design change, what position did the Patriots helmet patriot play?
10. Why did the Rams have the initials CR on their uniforms in SB XIV?

UNIFORMS
Answers

1.   It reflected the seven years of taunting the AFL had received as the more inferior league. Alas, it was proven to be right as the Packers won 35-10.
2.   Los Angeles Raiders and Miami Dolphins
3.   Los Angeles Rams in 1948.
4.   Seven, the Bills, Dolphins, Bengals (tiger stripes), Broncos, Eagles, Redskins (Indian headdress feathers), and the Rams.
5.   The Denver Broncos.
6.   The right eye.
7.   The Bears, with 13.
8.   To signify the ten-year history of the AFL in their last super battle before the merger between the two leagues was complete.
9.   Center.
10.   In honor of team owner Carroll Rosenbloom who drowned in the Atlantic Ocean in April, 1979.

VICTORIES
Questions

1.   Two head coaches have led their team to three SB victories. Who are they?
2.   Which was the first team to have two SB victories back-to-back?
3.   After Green Bay, which was the first team to be victorious in its first appearance at a SB?
4.   Which was the first NFL/NFC team to have three SB game victories?
5.   After Vince Lombardi's two Green Bay wins, who was the first coach to put together two consecutive SB victories?
6.   Who was the first NFC-NFL coach to have two consecutive victories, after Lombardi?
7.   Which is the only team to have back-to-back victories, twice?
8.   Of the teams scoring first, how many have been victorious?
9.   Of the teams leading at the half, how many have gone on to win?
10.   Which coach has the most victories?

VICTORIES
Answers

1. Bill Walsh of the San Francisco 49ers in XVI, XIX, and XXIII; Joe Gibbs, Washington Redskins, XVII, XXII, and XXVI. George Seifert coached the 49ers in their two other wins in XXIV and XXIX.
2. Green Bay Packers, SB I and II.
3. The New York Jets, SB III.
4. San Francisco 49ers, in SB XVI, XIX, and XXIII. Of course, they then went on to win five SB titles. Pittsburgh had three victories before Dallas, but they were AFL/AFC.
5. Don Shula, with Miami in SB VII and VIII.
6. Jimmy Johnson, Dallas Cowboys, in SB XXVII and XXVIII.
7. Pittsburgh Steelers, in IX, X, XIII, and XIV.
8. 22 of the 30 games.
9. There was one half-time tie, and 22 of the other 29 games have been won by the half-time leader.
10. Although the 49ers and the Cowboys have five victories, they were under the leadership of different coaches. Therefore, the answer is Chuck Noll, with four, for the Pittsburgh Steelers.

WOMEN
Questions

1. Who was the only woman to toss the Super Bowl coin?
2. Leslie Easterbrook sang the National Anthem for SB XVII. On what popular television sitcom did she appear as Rhonda Lee from 1980 to 1983?
3. Who is the only female owner of an NFL team to have gone to the Super Bowl?
4. Who are the Jills?
5. Who choreographed the Starbrites, the cheering squad for the Miami Dolphins, in their 1978 debut?
6. Which team was cheered on by the Liberty Belles?
7. What happened to the Ben-Gals, the cheerleading squad for the Cincinnati Bengals, in 1987?
8. Which ESPN skating commentator played the part of Snoopy at the SB XXIV half-time festivities?
9. What percentage of the television viewing audience is women?
    a) 25%   b) 33%   c) 40%   d) 50%
10. What was the name of the Denver cheerleading squad?

WOMEN
Answers

1. Marie Lombardi, widow of Vince Lombardi, in Super Bowl XV.
2. *Laverne and Shirley.*
3. Georgia Frontiere is the owner of the Los Angeles Rams.
4. The cheerleading squad for the Buffalo Bills.
5. June Taylor, known for her dancers on the Jackie Gleason television show.
6. The Philadelphia Eagles. Proceeds of a Central Penn National Bank poster of Belles Judy Duke, Carolyn Dawkins, Nancy Fanslau, Tammy Everngham and Betty Anne Messina went to the Eagles Fly For Leukemia Charity.
7. The only cheerleading squad in the American Football Conference Central division, they were disbanded, with the team noting the waning interest in cheers.
8. Judy Sladky, a 4'11" champion ice dancing skater.
9. c) Women comprise 40% of the viewing audience.
10. The Pony Express.

Xs & Os
Questions

1. Which running back passed for a touchdown in Super Bowl XII?
2. Which wide receiver passed for 23 yards in Super Bowl XXII?
3. In the second half of SB XIV wide receiver Ron Smith caught a TD to take the Rams into a 19-17 lead. Who threw the ball to him?
4. What was unusual about the way the Vikings executed their Xs and 0s in the first half of SB IX, scoring the only points of the first half?
5. What was unusual about Terry Brown scoring for the Minnesota Vikings in SB IX?
6. The Redskins have this place kicker to thank for their only TD in SB VII. What's his name?
7. What was unusual about William "The Refrigerator" Perry's TD in SB XX?
8. Which play assured a Pittsburgh victory in Super Bowl XIII?
9. In the land of Xs & Os and other letters, which SB QB won the state high school typing contest, when he was the only guy against 300+ girls?
10. Which US President called a coach to suggest a down-and-out play from Bob Griese to Paul Warfield?

Xs & Os
Answers

1. Robert Newhouse passed to Golden Richards for a 29-yard TD in the fourth quarter. It was the first pass thrown by Newhouse since 1975.

2. Steve Sewell to John Elway, during the Broncos second possession.

3. The Steelers were startled when halfback Lawrence McCutcheon appeared to be running an end sweep, and then McCutcheon pulled up and threw to Ron Smith.

4. The Vikings were at their own 10-yard line when a fumbled handoff caused the ball to bounce backwards, QB Tarkenton fell on it, sliding into the end zone and Dwight White downed him. The defensive team of the Steelers scored the safety.

5. Matt Blair broke through the Pittsburgh line to block Bobby Walden's punt and Viking Terry Brown pounced on it in the end zone for six points.

6. Garo Yepremian, trying to recover his own bad kick ended up passing the ball into the hands of Redskins' Mike Bass who ran in for a TD.

7. Perry normally filled a defensive slot on the Chicago Bears team.

8. Rocky Bleier recovered an onside kick with one second remaining to seal the Steelers' victory.

9. Troy Aikman.

10. Nixon called Dolphins coach Don Shula at 1:30 a.m. for the upcoming SB VI which the Dolphins lost to the Cowboys by a score of 24-3.

YARDS
Questions

1. Who holds the record for rushing yards in a single Super Bowl game?
2. Which QB holds the record for the most passing yards in a single SB game?
3. Which receiver carries the record for the most receiving yards in a single SB game?
4. After Montana and Bradshaw who had four SB games each, which QB is third in line for the most yards gained during his SB career?
5. What is the record for the most net yards gained by one team in a single Super Bowl game?
6. What is the record for the fewest net yards gained by a team in one Super Bowl game?
7. What is the record for the most yards gained by both teams in a single Super Bowl game?
8. What is the record for the fewest yards by both teams in a Super Bowl game?
9. Who holds the dubious title of the fewest rushing yards by a single team?
10. Okay, so maybe that was a fluke. What was the next lowest number of rushing yards?

YARDS
Answers

1. Timmy Smith, in SB XXII with 204 yards, Redskins against the Broncos.
2. Montana, in SB XXIII, with 357 when the 49ers wiped out the Bengals.
3. Jerry Rice, 49ers against the Bengals in SB XXIII.
4. Jim Kelly, with 829 yards, in his four games for Buffalo.
5. 602 yards by Washington against Denver, Super Bowl XXII.
6. The Vikings, with 119 yards, against the Steelers in SB IX.
7. 929 yards, by the Redskins and the Broncos in Super Bowl XXII.
8. 452 yards, by the Vikings and the Steelers, again in Super Bowl IX.
9. The New England Patriots when the Bears drubbed them in SB XX.
10. That was the Vikings, again, against the Steelers, with 17 yards, in SB IX.

ZEBRAS
Questions

1. What's the record number for the most officials ever to be on a field for a game?
2. How many officials work the game these days?
3. Who authored *Close Calls*, a book that detailed his experiences as an NFL referee?
4. Who is the one referee who has worked four Super Bowl games?
5. Which three others have been referee three times each?
6. Was there ever a SB call that the NFL ever said was wrong, which might have had an effect on the final outcome of the game?
7. Which was the first SB game to use a side judge and do you remember who it was?
8. Who is the one line judge who has worked five Super Bowl games?
9. Who is the only man to be Referee for SB games two years in a row?
10. Which SB game was the first to use Instant Replay and who was the Replay Official?

ZEBRAS
Answers

1. In SB I there were 12 officials on the field. Six worked the game, while the other six were held as alternates for each position. Half were from the AFL and the other half from the NFL.
2. Seven officials, with two alternates.
3. Norm Schachter.
4. Jerry Markbreit who completed his 19th year during the 1994-95 season. He was referee in the 1983 and 1987 games in Pasadena and the 1992 game in Minneapolis. He is president of the Officials Union, but that post is not pertinent to his selection as SB referee.
5. Referees Norm Schacter, Jim Tunney, and Pat Haggerty.
6. Yes. In SB XIII, referee Fred Swearingen called a 33-yard pass interference against Dallas defensive back Benny Barnes, giving the Steelers a last quarter possession at the Dallas 23. Four plays later, the Steelers scored, increasing its lead to 28-17. Steelers eventually won 35-31.
7. SB XIII, Dean Look, who would work as line judge in two subsequent games, Super Bowls XVI and XXVIII.
8. Jack Fette.
9. Jim Tunney.
10. SB XXIV, Al Sabato, who was also the line judge for SB I and the linesman for SB VI.

QUESTION

Do you have a question or piece of trivia that should be included in the next edition of *Super Bowl Trivia*? Please send it to:

Tuff Turtle Publishing
Box 3308
Crofton, MD 21114-0308

If you're the first person to submit the question and it's used, you'll receive a free copy of the book.

NEED MORE COPIES?

If you need more copies of *Super Bowl Trivia* because you think they'd make terrific gifts, or your friends keep taking your copy, send a check for $17.45 ($14.95 plus $3.50 for shipping and handling; $1 for s & h per copy after one, going to the same address) to:

Tuff Turtle Publishing
Box 3308
Crofton, MD 21114-0308

ORDER FORM
(please print)

Please send _____ copies of *Super Bowl Trivia* to:

_____

Name

_____

Address

_____

City, State, and Zip Code

A check for $_____ is enclosed.

_____ copies @ $14.95 each   _____
shipping $3.50 for 1st book   _____
shipping $1.00 for each additional book

                                       _____
Total   _____